W9-CJX-982

HEILONGJIANG

● Harbin

JILIN

● Changchun

● Shenyang

LIAONING

.R. (Inner Mongolia)

HEBEI

Hohhot

Beijing ■

● Tangshan

● Dairen

NORTH KOREA

Tianjin

Yaiyuan

SOUTH KOREA

SHANXI

Jinan

● Qingdao

SHANDONG

Yellow River

Kaifeng

Zhengzhou

XI

HENAN

Hefei

● Nanjing

● Shanghai

HUBEI

Wuhan

Hangzhou

Ningbo

ZHEJIANG

ng

Changsha ●

● Nanchang

● Wenzhou

HUNAN

JIANGXI

FUJIAN

● Fuzhou

West River

GUANGDONG

Taipei

XI A.R.

Guangzhou

● Xiamen

TAIWAN

Pacific Ocean

● Hong Kong

Macau

South China Sea

PHILIPPINE ISLANDS

HAINAN

JAPAN

GUANGDONG
CHINA'S PROMISED LAND

REGIONAL DEVELOPMENT IN CHINA

VOLUME 1

GUANGDONG

CHINA'S PROMISED LAND

EDITED BY **BRIAN HOOK**

HONG KONG
OXFORD UNIVERSITY PRESS
OXFORD   NEW YORK
1996

Oxford University Press

Oxford New York
Athens Auckland Bangkok Bombay
Calcutta Cape Town Dar es Salaam Delhi
Florence Hong Kong Istanbul Karachi
Kuala Lumpur Madras Madrid Melbourne
Mexico City Nairobi Paris Singapore
Taipei Tokyo Toronto

and associated companies in
Berlin Ibadan

Oxford is a trade mark of Oxford University Press

First published 1996

This impression (lowest digit)
1 3 5 7 9 10 8 6 4 2

Published in the United States
by Oxford University Press, New York

© Oxford University Press 1996

British Library Cataloguing in Publication Data
available

Library of Congress Cataloging-in-Publication Data
Guangdong : China's promised land / edited by Brian Hook.
    p.   cm. — (Regional development in China ; v. 1)
Includes bibliographical references and index.
ISBN 0–19–586180–9 (alk. paper)
1. Kwangtung Province (China)   2. Kwangtung Province (China)—
Economic conditions.   I. Hook, Brian.   II. Series.
HC428.K9G77   1996
330.51'27—dc20   96–33943
                                                           CIP

Printed in Hong Kong
Published by Oxford University Press (China) Ltd
18/F Warwick House, Taikoo Place, 979 King's Road, Quarry Bay, Hong Kong

FOREWORD

The changes that have taken place in China in the sixteen years since the reform programme began are staggering, and have brought about a dramatic transformation in the way hundreds of millions of people in China live their daily lives. Nowhere is this more apparent than in Guangdong and Fujian provinces, which are at the forefront of change in China. This book is a comprehensive and erudite guide to the history, geography, and development of Guangdong province, and will be an invaluable reference to those wishing to acquire a deeper understanding of this dynamic corner of the world's most populous country. I am confident that the other volumes planned for this series will match the high standards set in the first two volumes.

Smith New Court is proud to have assisted in a small way with the preparatory work for this book, and would like to congratulate the authors, editors, and publishers on a splendid achievement.

RICHARD MARGOLIS
Director, Smith New Court Plc
Hong Kong
July 1995

PREFACE

For almost three decades after the founding in 1949 of the People's Republic of China (PRC), the new political–economic system imposed a degree of conformity and egalitarianism that shrouded much of the country's regional diversity and economic disparity. Regional diversity and economic disparity could, however, never be wholly eliminated, nor, in the case of the former, was it ever the intention to do so. Once the PRC was firmly established there was nevertheless an impression of imposed uniformity and structured conformity rooted in policies such as land reform and the subsequent socialist transformation of agriculture, together with policies to transform capitalist industry and commerce. These trends were concurrently reflected in the output of the media, in the field of literature, and in the arts.

The remarkable degree of national conformity that had apparently been successfully imposed by the late 1950s periodically came under critical scrutiny and attack—particularly during the Cultural Revolution in the 1960s—for allegedly engendering deviation, subversion, provincialism, and localism. Even so, until the death of Chairman Mao Zedong in 1976, the PRC remained, despite the bitter inner Party and power struggles of the previous decade, a markedly monolithic and conformist state, the lives of whose citizens were characterized by an increasingly threatened uniform level of subsistence egalitarianism. In the course of those three decades, much of the underlying rich regional diversity, expressed in the history, culture, politics, economics, and geography of each region, was temporarily obscured as a direct consequence of the political–economic policies associated with Marxist-Leninism and Mao Zedong Thought.

Since the adoption of modernization policies following the rehabilitation and accession of Deng Xiaoping, the inherited Maoist system has undergone a great change. The nature and extent of the change is captured by the phrases the 'Four Modernizations' (agriculture, industry, science and technology, and national defence), 'socialism with Chinese characteristics', and 'the building of a socialist market economy'. The key aspect of what has amounted to a systemic change appears to be the promotion of a largely economic modernization programme, while maintaining certain socialist policies, and, moreover, the ability to repel any challenge to such policies through an unreconstructed Leninist one-party state system, as was evident in the crisis of 1989.

Although there have been challenges and vicissitudes, the policies of reform and opening out remain the basis for the unprecedented economic changes throughout the PRC. The most conspicuous have been in regions of China that have attracted significant levels of foreign investment, such as the provinces of Guangdong and Fujian, and the centrally administered municipalities of Shanghai, Tianjin, and Beijing. Viewed from an international perspective, within the Pacific Rim there have been movements of capital, producer goods, and human resources through Hong Kong and Taiwan, and from Japan and South Korea, contributing to a prodigious growth in fixed assets in and exports from Guangdong, Fujian, Shanghai, Tianjin, Beijing, and Liaoning. The level of development generated by foreign capital investment has inevitably focused most attention on these particular regions and cities. Many adjoining regions, and even those located at a greater distance from the centres of development, have been affected, directly or indirectly, by the policies of reform and opening out that have characterized the Deng Xiaoping initiatives.

These initiatives and the consequential systemic change in the PRC have had three major results. The first is the contribution throughout the country to the establishing of an irreversible trend towards national modernization, and the fulfillment of the quest—embarked upon a century earlier by Yan Fu and his contemporaries—for national wealth and power. The second is the demise of imposed conformity, and the re-emergence of regional diversity in its multifarious manifestations within the unified Chinese state system—a regional diversity which, in turn, determines both the potential for and the priority accorded to development in the newly established socialist market system. The third is a universal awareness among the growing constituencies in government, business, and academe who have interests in a particular region of China of the scarcity of authoritative writing on the regions of the PRC.

It seems certain that this search for wealth and power will continue. It follows that the regional diversity of China will become an increasingly crucial factor in ultimately determining the order, form, and magnitude of regional development as the concept of comparative advantage among the regions is exploited in the process of modernization. In these circumstances the modernization programme has inevitably generated a growing demand for an authoritative, up-to-date, and accessible source of information on the history and culture, government and politics, natural and human resources, and economic development of the regions. I hope that the Oxford University Press series on regional development in China will help to meet this need.

The launching of this series reflects three major developments in the Deng Xiaoping period. First, by removing the stifling shroud of Maoist political–economic conformity and uniformity, China can begin to exploit the productive forces latent in its rich regional diversity. Second, as a result of this emergence, it is no longer acceptable to infer from studies of one particular region or of the centre of China what conditions might be in other regions: it is essential now, for reasons of accuracy and reliability, to take account of regional individualism. Third, against a background of unprecedented development, millions of foreign visitors, among them many Chinese from Hong Kong, Macau, and Taiwan, and from the diaspora in Singapore, Malaysia, Thailand, and Indonesia, visit

China annually—a significant proportion on business. Their destinations are no longer confined to a mere handful of open cities, but are located throughout the regions, extending the length and breadth of the country. We hope that the studies published in this series will serve this large constituency.

The series, in which eight books are at present planned, is launched with the publication of two volumes, the first on Guangdong and the second on Fujian. These are to be followed by Volumes III and IV on Shanghai and the Yangtze Delta, and Beijing and Tianjin. Subsequent books are planned to cover the north-east, Taiwan, the north-west, and the south-west. The structure of each book is designed to enable the reader to proceed either sequentially from chapter to chapter, or to take a more modular approach by reading individual chapters in no prescribed order. There is clearly some advantage to be gained by the former approach, but, since some readers will have interests only in a particular aspect of the region, each author has attempted to make his chapter reasonably self-standing. An inevitable consequence of this is occasionally a modest level of overlap.

In creating and developing the series so far I would like to record my gratitude for the encouragement and help from colleagues in the Department of East Asian Studies at the University of Leeds, and from the staff of the Robert Black College and Centre for Asian Studies at the University of Hong Kong, the Universities Service Centre of the Chinese University of Hong Kong, and the recently established David C. Lam Institute for East–West Studies at the Hong Kong Baptist University. I wish to express my particular thanks to Mr Richard Margolis, Managing Director of Smith New Court Hong Kong, for his generosity in supporting the peer-review conference for the first two volumes, and to my wife Beth for her constant encouragement and help.

BRIAN HOOK
Department of East Asian Studies
The University of Leeds

CONTENTS

FIGURES AND TABLES

FIGURES

TABLES

CONTRIBUTORS

Robert F. Ash is a Senior Lecturer in Economics at the School of Oriental and African Studies at the University of London where from 1986 until 1995 he was also Director of the Contemporary China Institute. He is co-editor, with Y. Y. Kueh, of *The Chinese Economy Under Deng Xiaoping* (1996) and *Economic Trends in Chinese Agriculture: The Impact of Post-Mao Reforms* (1993). He has also published many articles on various aspects of China's economic development. Since 1982, he has compiled the 'Quarterly Chronicle and Documentation', published in the *China Quarterly*.

Richard Louis Edmonds is Director of the Contemporary China Institute and a Senior Lecturer in the Department of Geography at the School of Oriental and African Studies, University of London. Dr Edmonds has also taught at the University of Hong Kong and the Universidade de Macau, and was a student in the United States, Taiwan, and Japan. He has written books and articles on the geography of China and Japan including *Patterns of China's Lost Harmony: A Survey of the Country's Environmental Degradation and Protection* and *Macau* in the World Bibliography series.

David Faure works on the history of the Pearl River Delta and on Chinese business history. He has written *The Structure of Chinese Rural Society, Lineage and Village in the Eastern New Territories, Hong Kong* (1986); *The Rural Economy of Pre-Liberation China* (1989); and co-edited, with Helen F. Siu, *Down to Earth: The Territorial Bond in South China* (1995).

He is currently University Lecturer in Modern Chinese History, and Fellow of St Antony's College at the University of Oxford.

Brian Hook is a senior member of the academic staff of the University of Leeds where he teaches in the Department of East Asian Studies. He was a founder member of the original Department of Chinese Studies of which he was head between 1979 and 1982, and from 1985 to 1988. Between 1958 and 1963 he was a member of HMOCS in the Government of Hong Kong, serving as Assistant Secretary in the Secretariat for Chinese Affairs, and subsequently in the Colonial Secretariat. From 1980 to 1991, he was Editor of *The China Quarterly*. He has edited both editions of *The Cambridge Encyclopedia of China*. In 1995 he was University Fellow and Visiting Professor at the David C. Lam Institute for East–West Studies. His chief interest is the history of the People's Republic of China, and his recent publications examine the arrangements for the retrocession of Hong Kong, on which he plans a full-length study.

Y. Y. Kueh is Professor of Economics and Dean of the Faculty of Social Sciences at Lingnan College, Hong Kong. He has previously taught at the Chinese University of Hong Kong; Western Michigan University; Hong Kong Bapist University; and Macquarie University, Sydney, Australia, where he was Professor and Foundation Director of the Centre for Chinese Political Economy. He has been a Visiting Fellow at Harvard University and at the School of Oriental and African Studies in London. He is author/co-editor of *Agricultural Instability in China, 1931–1991* (1995), *Economic Trends in Chinese Agriculture: The Impact of Post-Mao Reforms* (1993), *The Chinese Economy under Deng Xiaoping* (1996), and of some forty articles on various aspects of economic change in China, and Chinese economic policy issues.

Lee Wing On is Director of the Comparative Education Research Centre at the University of Hong Kong. His major research interest is studying the implications of aspects of social change on education development. He is the author of *Social Change and Educational Problems in Japan, Singapore, and Hong Kong* (1991), co-editor of *Social Change and Educational Development: Mainland China, Taiwan, and Hong Kong* (1995), and editor of *The Development of Moral Education in China: A Documentary Analysis, a Special Issue of the Chinese Education and Society* (forthcoming). He is at present coordinating the IEA Civic Education Study in Hong Kong.

Winston **Ng Kwan Wai** is in the Department of Politics and Public Administration at the University of Hong Kong.

Elfed **Vaughan Roberts** lectures in the Department of Politics and Public Administration at the University of Hong Kong. He is co-author of *A Political Dictionary for Hong Kong* (1990), *Historical Dictionary of Hong Kong and Macau* (1992), and has a written numerous articles and chapters in the general field of Asian politics.

1 HISTORY AND CULTURE

David Faure

Guangdong's history evolved around the geography that was shaped by its rivers and the fact that it was the southernmost coastal province from Beijing. Its cities grew on the rivers. Its trade went along them and the coast. Its food supply came from the land that the rivers formed by dumping sediments into the shallow inlets that were at one time their estuaries. The rivers and their drainage basins have also become the confines of dialect regions: the Cantonese occupy most of the drainage area of the Pearl River and its tributaries, the Hakka the upland of the Han from where they moved, insidiously, so it would seem, down the East River, and the Chaozhou (Chiuchow) the lower reaches of the Han. If the Cantonese dialect is spoken all the way up the West River into Guangxi province, that is because historically the West had been a principal trade route. For centuries, these dialects defined civilization. Cantonese, Hakka, and Chaozhou have, at least since the 1400s, been regarded as variants of the Han language. Speakers of these dialects were wetland cultivators, adept at village and workshop industries, literate and centralized, willing to trade with barbarians and other Han-speakers alike, and for this reason, susceptible to influences coming from other parts of as well as from outside China. However, because of their distance from the centre, they were tolerably unorthodox. These southerners were ill-cultured rather than hard to govern, unusual enough to adapt readily to change but were settled far enough from the centre not to upset stability.[1]

THE HAN INFLUENCE

The Han people, Cantonese, Hakka, or Chaozhou, say that they had come into this region as outsiders. The official history records the conquest of the Lingnan (the southern hills) in the Qin dynasty (221–207 BC), from which time the city of Guangzhou was established. Thereafter, it was a history of acculturation and migration: the conversion of Chaozhou by the exiled scholar-official Han Yu (768–824) in the Tang dynasty (618–906), and the southward movement of the Cantonese as well as the Hakka families from the Song dynasty (960–1279). This reconstruction of the coming of the Han people leaves a rather uncomfortable gap of some twelve centuries during which the ethnic status of Guangdong inhabitants was kept in limbo. As far as the records can be made to tell the story: there were Han administrators in Guangzhou and Chaozhou, but beyond, it was a no man's land of curious creatures, monsters, monks, and eccentrics.

The trick the records play on the observer is, of course, the trick of writing. That is, the abundance of it in Guangzhou city, and its almost total absence beyond until the Song. Guangzhou had, from time immemorial, been a seaport. Geography supported its privilege, for the city was located at the highest point of the sunken valley that was the Pearl. From the early days of the Qin and Han dynasties (206 BC–220 AD), Guangzhou was known for its exotics. As late as the Han dynasty, elephants and rhinoceros roamed on the edges of the Pearl, and in the Tang, Han Yu was credited with his sacrifice to the crocodiles of Chaozhou. Traders came from afar for its tropical produce. Among them were Indians and Arabs, bringing their own religion. As for local produce, some parts of coastal Guangdong were well known for their pearls, the gathering of which was managed on and off as an imperial monopoly, and people, the trade in which was found to be so barbarous that officials worked hard to stamp it out. Guangzhou was a frontier town where civilizations met. Our written records preserve its history as viewed by the one group that had access to writing, and that, naturally, defined the writers' presence as the civilizing process.[2]

Whatever one might think of the meaning of civilization, however, it is beyond dispute that from early times, except for two brief periods, Guangdong has been an administrative division of the Chinese empire. The emperor appointed the senior local officials, who, in the style of officialdom developed since the Tang dynasty, encouraged the teaching of the Confucian classics, promoted schools, and reformed local customs in ways that made them more acceptable to orthodox creeds. Religion might have played an important part in the cultural conversion of Guangdong in the Tang and the Song, as the monasteries founded in this heyday of Buddhism that are still extant would testify. It is probably not unfair to say that the local inhabitants of Guangdong were Buddhist before they were Daoist, and Daoist before they were Han, that is, Chinese.

The Han influence was consolidated only in the Ming dynasty (1368–1644) and it came about partly because the imperial centre of the Ming successfully came to terms with the village structure of local society in the rice-growing parts of China, and partly because of the impact of economic development in the sixteenth century. There were two components to the Ming dynasty administrative philosophy that provided the meeting ground of state and society. The one dealt with taxation: how much tax should be collected, how it was to be collected, and by whom. Land and household registration was introduced in the early Ming; it was never implemented in full, but enough to ensure that county officials were supported by a regular income and that many people would have benefited from tax-sheltering activities. The other dealt with the provision of official titles and statuses, the most prestigious of which were granted in connection with the imperial examinations held every few years. Social mobility created by registration and examination can be vividly traced in ancestral records: the households that registered in the early Ming produced descendants that sat the imperial examinations by the mid-Ming, and the official status awarded to the successful scholar by association benefited his immediate relatives. Even the village landscape was changing. Where the Buddhist monastery in the Song had provided the focus of local organization, there now were built ancestral halls in a style that was legally defined and restricted to those families in which some claim might be made to senior official status. The symbolism of gentry society was coming into being, where all was well under heaven as long as the scholars remained in control and demonstrated filial piety to their ancestors and loyalty to the emperor. No historian should make the mistake that Guangdong society had always been so organized.[3]

TRADE AND THE OPENING OF GUANGDONG

One of the most prominent Guangdong gentry families in the Ming dynasty was the family of Huo Tao (1487–1540), which hailed from the edge of Foshan, an industrial town about ten miles west of Guangzhou. The ancestral hall was built in 1525, by Huo Tao himself while he was one of most senior ministers of the realm. His son Yuxia (1522–98) was a reputable scholar in his own right, having been a student of Zhan Ruoshui, one of the most noted philosophers of the sixteenth century and a very senior official as well. In Huo Tao's papers, we have his comments on the barbarian traders the *folangji*, known to Westerners as the Portuguese: 'The south-eastern barbarians paid their tribute from Guangzhou, and trade arose from this to the advantage of the market. In opposing it, the central state must not back itself into a corner. However, the *folangji* barbarians are the fiercest of bandits. They must be opposed.'[4] The statement reflects the negative sentiments that could always be detected in the official view towards Western trade, as obvious in the sixteenth century as later. Just as obvious, however, was the profitability of the trade that the Portuguese brought. Huo Tao's son Yuxia noted, perhaps in 1586, 'The treasures deposited by barbarian boats at Aomen (Macau) are heaped into a mountain, and all taxation is administered by the county magistrate. If he would only touch it lightly with his fingers, the income so derived would not be insubstantial.'[5]

It is useful to begin with a longer term view. Although it should be obvious Guangzhou had been engaged in trade since time immemorial, a shift in the trading pattern had occurred in the Southern Song when the imperial capital was moved to Hangzhou, near the delta of the Yangtze River. The move may be regarded as the culmination of a period of population growth and economic development of the lower Yangtze that had begun from the later Tang, say the ninth century. It also represented a major shift in the principal long-distance trade routes in which the imperial court took an interest, for while the Tang capital, Chang'an, was located at the end of the overland Silk Road from central Asia, the Southern Song was a maritime power, deriving considerable income from its sea-ports. The need to supply the new capital and its surround-ings with rice coupled with the increase in maritime trade brought about considerable development on the south China coast, although much of that was concentrated in Fujian rather than Guangdong. Chaozhou, located on the edge of Guang-dong adjacent to Fujian, benefited from that wave of eco-nomic expansion. Guangzhou was, therefore, very much in the backwaters. None the less, thanks to the expansion in the rice trade, land reclamation was begun on the Pearl River Delta. It was the development of an internal market for grain rather than the continuation of a luxury market in exotics that propelled Guangdong into the economic development that characterized much of the Ming and the Qing.

We might justifiably wonder how trade was conducted in these early days in the Ming dynasty, both among the Chinese themselves and between Chinese and foreigners, that is, Arabs and South-East Asians before the Portuguese appeared on the scene. The trade in exotics was different from the trade in staples first in terms of scale. Grain production opened up the river valleys and deltas. In the first instance it was conducted by the producers themselves in open markets. It was conta-gious: the urban markets were almost insatiable and uncultivated 'waste' land was brought into cultivation as the market

5

expanded. Reclamation called into question land rights, which were best established by registering at least some land and some household members, living or deceased, with the government. The government was prepared to support land rights that might be established by written deeds, the writing of which brought into existence village handbooks of daily affairs. The economic culture that was generated by the growth of a pervasive market was endemic. Ming dynasty rural trade in Guangdong or elsewhere in China was not confined to a class of merchants. In most of lowland Guangdong, there probably were few villages that were more than a day's journey from a local market at which villagers sold their produce.[6]

Yet surely there were merchants. Whoever managed the industries in a town such as Foshan, that became well known in the Ming dynasty for its iron as well as its pottery and silk? What we know of these traders suggests that the distinction between the merchant and the villager was considerably fluid, but the distinction between natives and outsiders was quite real. How deeply ingrained commercialism was in the household claiming an official status may be gleaned from another Huo family regulation ascribed to possibly the sixteenth century: 'Storing up money is not as worthwhile as stocking up goods. . . . Do not stock what is hard to put away and damages easily, or what few people use. Such items as unbroken iron slabs from Foshan and unbroken pots from Shiwan are worth stocking.'[7] The gentry families of Foshan, such as Huo Tao's, owned the markets, ferries, kilns, and ironworks, as well as the land around them. But into Foshan came the outside merchants, including wealthy merchants from the provinces of Shanxi and Shaanxi in the north, who traded throughout China. Remains left by the outsiders must have dotted the Guangdong coast. The distance that merchants might travel away from home is well illustrated by an iron bell cast in 1697 in Foshan. It was donated by a man from as far away as Zhejiang province to the small temple dedicated to the Goddess of Heaven at the market town of Tuen Mun in the New Territories of Hong Kong.

As far as we can tell, government had little to do with the

carrying on of most items of trade. Among the exceptions was salt, which was managed as a government monopoly. This simply meant that merchants engaged in the trade were required to be licensed. The law also demanded that brokers pay a fee, although it is unclear how this was enforced. Then there was the foreign trade, regarded by long-established custom as a special category.

In the Ming dynasty, private overseas trade was banned. In effect, the ban simply reduced to smugglers and pirates all sea-going merchants, of whom there were many. There would have been, in any case, a thriving coastal trade between Guangdong and Fujian as well as further north. However, it seems from the sixteenth century that it was the Fujian merchants who plied between Nagasaki or Manila and the China coast, taking abroad Chinese porcelain, tea, and silk and returning with Japanese silver or copper, and New World silver brought to the Philippines by the Spanish. There was also the official trade, conducted as tribute. The tribute bearer landed at specified Chinese ports, of which Guangzhou was one, and arrangements were made for trade with the delivery of the tribute. These overseas merchants came and departed with the monsoon. They traded under their own headmen and were closely supervised by Chinese officials, who, as Huo Yuxia noted, collected taxes from them. The Portuguese, marked out from the beginning of their contact with the Chinese as troublemakers, were initially banned from the tributary trade. However, it seems that they bribed their way in, and made arrangements with local officials for permission to trade regularly at Macau from as early as 1553. Their presence has continued into the twentieth century.

Portuguese contact left two impressions on the Chinese, both of which are still discernible although Guangdong people have not stood out as impressionable observers. Through Macau came the Jesuit missionaries, the most famous of whom, Matteo Ricci, spent some time in Guangdong before proceeding to Beijing. Through Macau came also Western firearms. Towards the end of the Ming dynasty, the imperial government ordered cannon from Macau when it was desperate for weaponry to repel its Manchu assailants. The collapse of the Ming dynasty brought a short lull to trade, when the coast was evacuated for seven years between 1662 and 1668 to isolate coastal pirates and Ming loyalists. The revival of trade after the coastal evacuation brought back the previous prosperity many times over, unmistakably indicated by the circulation of Spanish dollars and creeping inflation throughout the eighteenth century in Guangdong and other parts of coastal China. However, in the eighteenth century, overseas trade was no longer dominated by the Portuguese. The balance of power in the West had changed, and on the scene were English merchants, soon followed by American.

As part of worldwide commercial expansion, there was much more trade in this part of Asia in the eighteenth century than before. However, it has to be recognized that eighteenth century overseas trade was similar to that of the sixteenth and seventeenth centuries in many respects. Much of the cargo that was carried in Western merchant boats to China had not originated in Europe, and the English participated as enthusiastically as the Portuguese in carrying on trade that linked India, South-East Asia, China, the Philippines, and Japan. Nor had the institutional basis for trading changed. Overseas traders were confined to their quarters, and this practice applied not only to English merchants in China, but also to Chinese merchants in the Philippines and Indonesia. The most noticeable change in the trading patterns came from Chinese restrictions. After a hopeful beginning under the reign of the emperor Kangxi (1662–1722), the imperial government steadily adopted a more cautious approach towards Westerners, with the result that not only was Christianity banned from China in 1727 but all trade with the West was from 1757 to be confined to Guangzhou. It was no longer possible to restrict trade to tribute, but the imperial government ruled that it was to be managed by licensed merchants. The employment of licensed merchants in China coincided with the rise of the chartered companies in the West but may be traced to a separate origin in the evolution of Chinese government monopolies. Looking at it from the vantage point of the two

Opium Wars in the nineteenth century, historians have regarded the conduct of trade between the licensed Guangzhou merchants, the Co-hong, and the 'country traders' trading under licence from the East India Company to be the heyday of Sino-Western trade before the mid-nineteenth century. It should be realized that that particular arrangement was the culmination of several centuries of development. China certainly was not 'opened' by the Opium War.[8]

The restriction of Western trade to Guangzhou brought to that city unprecedented prosperity. Never before had so much luxury been so obvious. The Co-hong merchants were among the richest people in the whole of China. Nearby Nanhai and Shunde counties produced the silk that was added to the import from the Yangtze delta for export to foreign countries. Consumption of food in the towns and the city fuelled a buoyant rural market. Foshan continued to manufacture its silk, pottery, and iron. The families that controlled landed estates built fine ancestral halls in the villages as well as in Guangzhou city. Performances at rituals held in these ancestral halls and other centres of wealth brought to life the Cantonese opera, as many operatic troupes were based at their guildhall at Foshan. The literati passed the imperial examination in larger numbers, but many must have also frequented the sing-song boats moored to the west of the city. The popular songs of the day sung by the 'sing-song girls' on these boats and written by the scholars were such fine Cantonese literature that Cecil Clementi, who was to serve as Governor of Hong Kong from 1925 to 1930, translated them into English.[9] The artistic tradition was represented by the painters Li Jian and Su Liupeng, whose styles were not only popular among upper-class artists in Guangzhou, but were also copied in mural paintings adorning the walls of village houses. The crowning glory of Guangzhou cultural life was the Xuehai Tang (Sea of Learning Hall) Academy, founded by Governor Ruan Yuan in 1820, himself one of the leading contemporary commentators of the classics. Early nineteenth-century Guangzhou was poised to shake off its backwater image. It never quite did that, for it was soon overshadowed by Shanghai and Hong Kong.

CENTRE AND PERIPHERY

The Western view conceives of changes in China as responses to a Western impact. The Han view conceives of changes in south China as the integration of local societies into a unified fold. There has never quite been a south China view. Guangdong was never the centre of any history. It is ironic how much happened in Guangdong that was of crucial importance to the overall political development of China even as Guangdong remained on the periphery.

The first Opium War (1840–2) is an example of how Guangdong must appear peripheral in order for an event to be explicable. Guangzhou was the southernmost seaport of scale throughout the Ming and the Qing, and it was the distance from the capital Beijing that recommended it as the port to which Western trade should be restricted. The Cantonese, except for a short period when Huo Tao and his associates were influential at court, did not wield great influence in the inner circles of imperial power, unlike the lower Yangtze literati or the Manchu aristocrats. Not since the philosopher Chen Baisha in the fifteenth century had they produced a scholarly figure with a statewide reputation. It is in this light that one can understand the appeasement of the English as the Opium War (1840–2) dragged on that prompted the imperial government to yield, among other things, the island of Hong Kong.

No one should dispute that the first Opium War was started because the English sold opium to China and the Chinese Imperial Commissioner, Lin Zexu, attempted to stop this illegal traffic in 1839, making it very clear to the foreigners that unless the drug was handed over, no trade might resume and, indeed, no foreign merchant might be safe. He had the support of some Guangdong scholars who had written popular tracts to warn of the danger of opium addiction to the empire. Lin, however, came from a small group of senior officials, many of whom had close lower Yangtze connections, who took a global view of administrative policies. Addiction to opium was a social evil, but just as important as this moral issue was the outflow of silver in return for the import of 'foreign mud'. The depletion of silver in China, they believed, made its value appreciate, and, because silver was one of the two common media of exchange (the other being copper coins), prices had become depressed while taxation, denominated in silver, had soared. The decision to ban the import of opium was a policy made in the interest of the state, and it was one in which the merchants of Guangzhou had little alternative but to acquiesce.

The British handed over the drug, but wrote home to ask for military support. However questionable the handling of the diplomatic situation might have seemed to the locals, when British guns bombarded Guangzhou and British (and Indian) troops appeared on Chinese soil, there was no question where the loyalty of the locals lay. The militia of the Guangzhou suburb had been mobilized, along with the militia of the entire China coast from Guangdong to Zhejiang, in preparation for the war. The militia of Sanyuanli village to the north of Guangzhou demonstrated their mettle as they held down a small company of British troops. Minor victories in small skirmishes notwithstanding, China lost the war, while Guangzhou came under bombardment as one of its principal theatres. Defeat did not impress upon the Cantonese, or the officials who governed them, that the English were invincible. Instead, it turned them against the West.[10]

An underlying anti-Western strain, often quite specifically anti-English, never quite disappeared from Guangzhou and its surroundings. It surfaced openly when the British, on the strength of the Treaty of Nanking reached at the end of the war, demanded to be allowed to settle in Guangzhou, and it occurred surreptitiously in common customs and understandings. The stone pillars of the temple devoted to the patron deity of one of the ironworkers' guilds at Foshan, the industrial-cum-commercial town near Guangzhou, had as part of its motifs an English soldier at its base supporting the weight of the pillar on his shoulders. The village priests of the New Territories of Hong Kong incorporated into their chants offered to the dead the description that the two sedan-chair bearers burnt as part of the funeral offering were foreigners, who would now presumably pay back in the underworld for whatever exploitation that had been exerted in this world. Despite such undertones, however, Guangzhou was not xenophobic. The wounded pride of the Cantonese did not erupt very often, and it did not erupt at all unless it was made part of a national issue.

Though the first Opium War has come to be seen as a turning point in modern Chinese history, to the generation that experienced the Treaty of Nanjing, foreign aggression was only one issue among the turmoil of the time. The Taiping Rebellion beginning in neighbouring Guangxi province swept through Guangdong like a whirlwind, unleashing local tensions that erupted into local warfare. Bandits and rebels sprang up in innumerable places, many joining the secret society known as the Triads. In Foshan, they declared the foundation of a new kingdom, donning theatrical costumes as court clothes. Meanwhile, the Hakka clashed with the Cantonese for territorial control in areas to the west of Guangzhou city, further extending the Hakka presence in Guangdong. In the midst of all this turmoil, the British and the French sought an excuse to go to war, capturing in one of their first victories in 1858 the city of Guangzhou and the governor-general of Guangdong and Guangxi. In this near state of anarchy, the senior gentrymen of Guangzhou organized defence.[11]

The leaders of this defence movement were gentrymen of silk-producing Shunde county to the west of Guangzhou. These were not the wealthy Co-hong merchants, the Co-hong monopoly having been abolished after the first Opium War, but wealthy land developers who had been reclaiming the local reaches of the delta. The local defence organizations, in a loose sense, were based on the communal 'schools', institutions so named not because they carried out any teaching, but because by definition the majority of gentrymen who wielded *de facto* local jurisdiction were imperial students and communal 'schools' were institutions that would have been acceptable to the imperial regime as centres of local organization. The imperial court was highly suspicious of the establishment of a local militia. In the early years of the nineteenth century, the Jiaqing emperor (1796–1820) had noted in response to requests for permission to organize a militia that if the local people were allowed to arm, they would no longer willingly pay their taxes. However, preparation for the first Opium War required the mobilization of coastal China, and by the time the regular army had failed to curb the Taiping rebels, it was a foregone conclusion that the militia had to be permitted.[12]

The immediate results of local militarization did not prove as detrimental to the imperial regime as had been feared. The central government did lose its control of the land tax, but that was made up for by the substantial increase in maritime customs that resulted from more of China being opened to Western trade. County and provincial governments derived considerable income from a transit tax on goods that was imposed from the time of the Taiping Rebellion. Stability resumed from the late 1860s to the end of the nineteenth century, broken only by another wave of heightened anti-foreign feelings in the early 1880s during the infamous Sino-French war, which took place in Vietnam and Fujian rather than Guangdong. Even the Boxer Rebellion in north China in the last years of the nineteenth century left Guangdong unscathed.

ECONOMIC PROSPERITY

In the decades following the Taiping Rebellion, Guangzhou was no longer the only port where overseas trade was permitted. This is not to say that trade declined. Quite the contrary, overseas trade, now carried by steamers arriving from Europe via the Suez Canal, reached unprecedented levels. However, since the 1870s, whatever success Guangdong enjoyed in this respect, it was Shanghai at the mouth of the lower Yangtze River that took the limelight.

Guangzhou was not comparable to Shanghai. The international settlement of Shanghai became the forerunner of Westernization in China, and the surrounding Chinese population grew as the international settlement shot into prominence.

Shanghai was its own port; its hinterland the whole of the Yangtze valley. The equivalent of the Shanghai international settlement in Guangzhou was Shameen (Shamian), a tiny island on the Pearl River set quite apart from the rest of Guangzhou city. However, the comparison of Guangzhou on its own to Shanghai is less than fair, for the port that imported and exported for the whole of the Pearl River Delta was not Guangzhou, but the British colony of Hong Kong, ceded to Britain after the first Opium War. Although Guangzhou and Hong Kong were 100 miles apart, the two cities were socially and economically very close. The population of Hong Kong came almost entirely from the Pearl River Delta. They were, like the population of Guangzhou, predominantly Cantonese. They read the same newspapers, some of which were published in Hong Kong. The same opera companies played in both cities. Chinese restaurants in Hong Kong claimed in their advertisements that their chefs had made their careers first in Guangzhou, just as Western sexuality made its inroad into Guangzhou from Hong Kong advertising.[13]

The mainstay of Guangdong exporting was silk, which accounted for half or more of the Pearl River Delta's exports abroad. Most of this silk came from Shunde and adjacent Nanhai county where silk farming was a specialized activity. Farmers grew mulberry trees and raised silk worms, tended the worms until they spun their cocoons, sold the cocoons to operators of silk 'filatures', where the silk thread was unwound from the cocoon and prepared for the export market. In former days, the filatures were not mechanized. By the 1880s, one of the first indications of industrialization in Guangdong, and, indeed, in the whole of China, came in the introduction of steam power to the filatures. The steam was used for heating: the cocoons had to be immersed in hot water before the thread was picked up by chopsticks skilfully manipulated by a female worker and tied onto a revolving roller driven not by steam power but the human foot operating on a treadle. The steam filature, a device by which a central source of steam provided the heat needed for a team of workers, brought about a revolution in silk preparation. Hand-reelers rioted when the steam filature was introduced into the Pearl River Delta, but the rioting did not prevent the device from being adopted. By the 1890s, more than half of Guangdong's silk export was produced by the steam filature.[14]

Next to silk, Guangdong's foreign-exchange earnings came from produce exported to Hong Kong. The booming city needed daily supplies of food and fuel, building materials, and labour. From across the border in Guangdong came fresh pork and firewood, scaffolding bamboo, sacrificial paper, mandarin oranges, dried persimmon, eggs, and the innumerable items that appeared regularly on the records of the Chinese Maritime Customs Service. None was exported in noticeable amounts on a national scale, but all reflected the complexities of social life in a city the population of which grew from 120,000 in the 1860s to 800,000 by 1930. It was characteristic of this predominantly Cantonese population that there was considerable movement back and forth between Hong Kong and the villages of the Pearl River Delta, noticeable crowds appearing at various festivals during which workmen in Hong Kong were given leave to return home. Payments made for goods imported from Guangdong into Hong Kong, and for the several products of Guangdong origin that were exported from Hong Kong, opened a flood of Hong Kong currency into Guangdong province. By the early years of the twentieth century, the twenty-cent piece from Hong Kong was standard currency in Guangdong and preferred to the various Chinese coins that came to be closely associated with repeated attempts at currency devaluation.

Yet another source of foreign-exchange earnings from the last decades of the Qing dynasty to the Chinese Republic came in the form of human labour abroad. Known as the coolie trade, the export of labour can be set in the context of long-established patterns of migration. Since the Ming, if not earlier, there had been continuous emigration from various parts of Guangdong and nearby Fujian to areas where land might be reclaimed for cultivation. The Hakka extension down the East River was as much a search for arable land as the Cantonese reclamation of the Pearl River Delta. The willingness to work

15

abroad was exploited early in the nineteenth century when Guangdong workmen were recruited to work on board steamers, and under indenture in mines, railways, and plantations in Malaya, Chile, Australia, and North America. The labourers were recruited by agencies under fixed-term contracts. Partial payment was made in advance, and the labourer served out his term under tight supervision. The trade aroused considerable suspicion from Western governments, which detected in it elements of slavery. It was also popularly thought that many who went abroad as indentured labourers had not done so willingly and never survived to return. However, mingled with all this was the establishment of Chinese businesses abroad. In the same way as Chaozhou merchants settled in trading communities scattered in Singapore, Saigon, and Bangkok, Cantonese and Hakka traded in areas to which they had gone as migrant labourers. The migrant with his new-found wealth from overseas was a common phenomenon before the end of the nineteenth century. The most prominent of these returned migrants were granted official titles by the Qing government in recognition for their industrial investments, but many more who had become wealthy on a more modest scale returned to build houses in the villages and to endow village welfare. The forty-mile Xinning Railway was built on private capital in 1909, at a time when developers from Hong Kong, themselves returned migrants, drew up plans for real estate projects that were to set up new ports on the Guangdong coast.[15]

The vibrant export-led economy prospered from the last decades of the nineteenth century practically non-stop until the early 1930s. The sudden demise of the international silk market brought much of Guangdong's prosperity to a stop, and that was coupled with the drying up of overseas remittances as The Great Depression hit the West. For a short period in the 1930s, like the rest of China, Guangdong came under a wave of government enthusiasm for economic planning, a process that brought to the fore the government-run sugar industry. War loomed by 1937, and that eclipsed economic prosperity as a central concern.[16]

CULTURE AND IDENTITY

At what stage in their long history did the people of Guang-dong think of themselves as such? Probably not very much before the sixteenth century, when the first Guangdong local record was compiled by a Guangdong native. Thereafter, the Guangdong identity had hardly ever remained unchanged, and with that came changes in the perception of Guangdong culture.

The question is not whether Guangdong had a unique cul-ture: the problem is whether Guangdong culture, unique or not, would have counted as 'culture'. In other words, by the time Guangdong people recognized themselves as distinct, how might they have put themselves on a par with other people in China?

They could not be identical with the rest of China. To begin with, they did not speak the same language. Cantonese, Chaozhou, and Hakka were, and are, not understandable to northerners. But social class might also have exacerbated eth-nic differences. Upper-class culture in dynastic China being closely defined in relation to scholarly pretensions, the cul-tural groups of Guangdong had to produce their own mem-bers of the literati if they were to be counted. The first scholar of stature to come out of Guangdong was the philosopher Chen Baisha in the fifteenth century. Chen taught a variety of neo-Confucianism which gave the individual a place in soci-ety that was mediated through 'quiet sitting', but almost as important as Chen's teaching was the intellectual affinity that he established among his students. Chen was among the most notable scholars of the Ming dynasty, as Qing writers of in-tellectual traditions would acknowledge. After Chen, it was not until the nineteenth century that Guangdong would pro-duce nationally-reputed interpreters of the classics.[17]

Interpretations of the classics, even when they were written by Guangdong people, did not produce a written culture embodying local colours. A written culture that incorporated localism emerged only in the nineteenth century: the songs sung by the 'sing-song girls', who were the subject matter of this literature, made no bid for high culture in the national or even the local literati scene. The Cantonese opera, which incorporated the music and singing styles developed in the songs, was always a hybrid. The operatic tradition had come into Guangdong from the north. In its early history—our records on this issue begin with the Ming—Chaozhou had a stronger local operatic tradition than Guangzhou, but even there, the local Chaozhou opera consisted of a blend of local colours with northern operas rather than an independent invention. In the eighteenth century, wealthy people in Guangzhou maintained private northern operatic companies, while local operatic companies performed to the wider audience. Only in the nineteenth century with the decline of the northern companies in Guangzhou did local companies take the lead in Cantonese operas, now incorporating more Cantonese songs into the performances. Until the Taiping Rebellion, the Cantonese opera companies were attached to their guild at Foshan. The guild hall was burnt during the rebellion, and Cantonese opera itself was banned on government orders because of the involvement of the operatic companies in uprisings. The Cantonese opera came into its own only when the ban was formally lifted in the 1870s.[18]

Cantonese never quite emerged as a written language, despite attempts to make written Cantonese a viable possibility. The market for Cantonese culture did expand as the Cantonese people moved into cities and abroad from the second half of the nineteenth century. Cantonese opera was performed in South-east Asia as in California in the early years of the twentieth century, and to ever-increasing theatre audiences in Hong Kong. Apart from the theatre, the late nineteenth century also saw the introduction into China of the daily press. The combination of an entertainment industry and a daily press geared towards the ordinary man, in turn, brought about popular fiction in which native dialect formed an essential part of written speech. Long before Cantonese songs were sung to an audience of millions on the television screen, Cantonese poetry was reproduced in Hong Kong newspapers and consumed also overseas in Cantonese communities and up the Pearl

River Delta in China. Finally, in the 1930s the Cantonese cinema appeared, in which Cantonese opera soon found a place. Who is to say that Tang Disheng, writing in the Golden Age of Cantonese opera in the 1950s in Hong Kong, is not to count among China's bards? Yet, Tang Disheng makes no appearance in any literature textbook. Chinese literature makes no concession for local traditions, despite the claims of cultural iconoclasm in the May Fourth Movement of 1919. Chinese literature remains Chinese, and Cantonese remains peripheral if not questionable.

TOWARDS THE NEW CHINA

China's defeat by Japan in 1895 and the military occupation of Beijing after the Boxer Uprising in 1900 ushered in a period of crisis and change. These events took place in north China, and for this reason, Guangdong escaped the direct brunt of their consequences. Nevertheless, the memories of defeat mingled with the openness of Guangdong did produce discontent among a minority that set its mind on overthrowing the imperial regime. As a result, Guangdong became caught in a political current that was unstoppable.

Birthplace of Revolution

In some ways, it was natural that Guangdong should have produced more than its share of radicals and revolutionaries. The proximity of Hong Kong proved the destabilizing factor. The British Crown Colony of Hong Kong was from early days regarded with a mixture of envy and anger by Chinese intellectuals. On the one hand, Hong Kong represented the success of imperialism, but, on the other hand, Hong Kong was one of China's windows on the rest of the world. Two features of Western society, as seen through Hong Kong, particularly contributed to the fall of the Chinese empire. First, in Hong Kong, as in the treaty ports on the China coast and in Western society itself, merchants as merchants stood up to government. Second, information flowed relatively easily

19

owing not to government policies, but to the widely perceived need for education, the missionary zeal for disseminating religious ideas, and the profits reaped by publishing newspapers.

Thus, a generation of Chinese people educated in Hong Kong, disillusioned with the weakness of the imperial government, protected from the reach of imperial law by Hong Kong's colonial status, somewhat naturally embraced radical political ideals by which they wanted to save China. Sun Yatsen, founder of the Chinese republic, who attended medical school in Hong Kong, was the most well known representative of these radicals, but Wu Tingfang, barrister, one-time Legislative Councillor in Hong Kong, and senior imperial official who defected early to the revolutionaries in 1911, would have been just as typical. Nevertheless, Hong Kong was not the hotbed of revolution it could have been. The Hong Kong government was wary of providing sanctuary for revolutionaries. Sun Yatsen himself was, for some time, *persona non grata* in Hong Kong.[19]

The revolution in 1911 began as an accident. The events that occurred in many parts of the country, Guangdong included, in response to the initial mutiny in Wuchang city in Hubei province came as the culmination of political energy unleashed since the Boxer Uprising of 1900. A crucial development from the Boxer Uprising and open warfare between the imperial court and foreign powers in China was the declaration of independence by the provinces on the Yangtze. In response to the perceived threat of secession by the senior officialdom in the provinces, the court instituted constitutional reforms. For the first time in Chinese history, officialdom was not to intercede between the emperor and his subjects, and instead, representative assemblies were to be formed by popular election that might counterbalance the administrative authority of appointed officials. The imperial government also abolished the examination system whereby officials had been selected. In less than a decade, the imperial government revamped the Chinese society that had coalesced since the early Ming dynasty. In Guangzhou, the top-heavy administrative apparatus dominated by the governor-general with the diffused support of the local gentry gave way to active participation in municipal and provincial politics by the guilds, the charitable associations and the chamber of commerce.[20]

As in other parts of China, railway building was the bone of contention in provincial political disputes. China's railway-building excitement came in the 1890s and continued into the early years of the twentieth century, coinciding with an investment mania stimulated by the realization that government control on economic development had been set aside in favour of market-led growth. The problem was not that funds for investment were insufficient. On the contrary, there was too much investment capital, especially in Guangdong. Hitherto, Chinese investors had been introduced to stocks and shares by Western companies that traded in China. By the turn of the twentieth century, with commercial and administrative reforms, Chinese companies were raising share capital on the open market, and they found ready clients among gentrymen, returned emigrants, and merchants. The political furore of the day was that China's railway development rights should not have been mortgaged to foreigners. The provincial elites of Guangdong, as in other provinces, were prepared to redeem what rights had been mortgaged and to build their own railways. In the initial stages marked by popular sentiments in favour of 'rights redemption', the central government was a bystander. However, when by 1911 the central government implemented various moves to bypass the provincial elite and centralize China's railway development, it became the target of all popular protests, led not by the rabble but by provincial gentrymen of high standing.

In Guangdong, the stand-off between the provincial gentrymen and the Guangdong governor-general had begun long before the first shot was fired in Wuchang. Sun Yatsen's revolutionary group, based in Hong Kong and Tokyo, had staged an uprising in Guangzhou city in March and a search was on for revolutionaries. The gentry and merchants, however, were more concerned with the shareholders' meeting of the Guangzhou–Hankou Railway and what appeared close to political persecution in connection with that event. The Guangzhou–Hankou Railway had been redeemed at substantial cost from the American China Development Company only now to be told that it would be nationalized. The shareholders at their meeting opposed the nationalization, and were supported by numerous chambers of commerce not only in Guangzhou but also in other cities in Guangdong. When the governor-general declared the decision of the shareholders null and void, they generated a run on the banks, in response to which the governor-general banned the publication of any view on the matter in the newspapers and arrested one of the journalists who had written strongly in opposition to nationalization. The shareholders moved their meeting to Hong Kong, and there appealed for support from the Guangdong provincial assembly. It was at this point that revolt broke out in Wuchang. Not surprisingly, the Guangdong gentry took the side that supported detaching the province from the imperial regime.[21]

The events of 1911 illustrate amply the dire consequences when the central government in Beijing lost its grip on the provincial leadership. However, if the central government paid for that weakness with its own survival, subsequent events were to show what befell the province with the collapse of national government. Guangzhou was a rich prize for any armed band that would maraud in the name of the revolution. The revolutionaries of 1911, with their sight on an elected parliament in Beijing, provided no viable provincial leadership. Although Yuan Shikai, Republican China's first president, appointed the revolutionary Hu Hanmin to the military governorship of Guangdong in 1912, Hu was removed quickly enough in 1913 when Yuan clamped down on parliamentary democracy and the revolutionaries rose in arms. In Hu's place was the first warlord to be appointed to the governorship of Guangdong, General Long Jiguang, who came into Guangdong with his army of Guangxi men. While stationed in Guangdong, the Guangxi men were in a position to raise taxes locally along with innumerable self-appointed local commanders who had rallied to the revolutionary cause.

The Warlord Years

The next ten years of the history of Guangdong were taken up by warlord politics. The Guangdong warlords were non-ideological. General Long Jiguang supported Yuan Shikai in his attempt to revive monarchy, and was ousted by General Lu Rongting who brought his own troops into Guangdong. Sun Yatsen introduced an ideological element into these power disputes. In the 1910s, his slogan was the 'defence of the constitution', referring to the constitution that was suspended in 1913 when Yuan Shikai dismissed parliament in Beijing. To force home his political point, Sun set up the national parliament in Guangzhou that was attended by a splinter group of members of parliament from 1917 but was himself ousted when the warlords of the southern provinces took over his slogan and turned the 'defence of the constitution' campaign to their own advantage. Lu Rongting was then ousted in 1920 under the slogan of 'Guangdong for the Guangdong people' by an alliance formed between Sun and the Guangdong warlord Chen Jiongming. The alliance did not last, for by 1922 Chen attempted to stage a *coup d'etat* from which Sun barely escaped with his life.

Sun, however, soon had the opportunity to build his own military base with the help of the Communist International (Comintern). The Comintern, through its agent Joffe, had approached Sun with assistance to rebuild the Kuomintang (Nationalist Party). The offer could not have come at a more urgent time. Military groups with only a loose sense of affiliation had turned against the Guangdong warlord Chen Jiongming, and Yunnan and Guangxi troops had returned to Guangzhou and stationed themselves in the city. Despite their apparent willingness to ally with him, Sun had absolutely no control over these armed bands. Meanwhile, the urban population of Guangdong and surrounding villages had become disgusted with the warring factions, arbitrary demands on their properties and the lack of protection against unruly troops. With the help of the Comintern, Sun Yatsen's party founded the Whampoa Military Academy in Guangzhou where an officer corps recruited from all over China could be trained. This became the focus of the military buildup to be deployed in the Northern Expedition to reunite the country. The involvement of the Comintern, and the forging of a social and nationalist programme by the Kuomintang brought popular movements in Guangdong to new heights.[22]

Though order reigned in most of Guangdong during the 1920s, no single group in the name of any government exerted much authority over a large section of the province. Instead, while the counties or even portions of individual counties fell under the control of local groups, Guangzhou and Hong Kong were increasingly gripped by demonstrations of ideological allegiance in the form of popular movements. The 1922 seamen's strike in Hong Kong was a precursor of such activities. Striking seamen retreated to Guangzhou where they were given safe sanctuary and from there brought the Hong Kong government to accept their demands for improved working conditions. From about the same time, and, begun under the auspices of warlord Chen Jiongming, a peasants' movement had been directed by ideologically minded and educated young men. The training school for organizers of the peasants' associations in Guangzhou, founded by Peng Bai, who pioneered the peasants' movement in Haifeng county, was for a short while run by none other than Mao Zedong. At the time Mao was a junior cadre of the newly founded Chinese Communist Party who, with other members, had been instructed by the Comintern to join the Guomindang in a personal capacity.

The obvious 'Bolshevism' of the Guomindang at this point in its history was viewed with great suspicion by the merchants of Guangzhou and the government of Hong Kong. It is still an open question if and how the Hong Kong government was implicated in the 'merchant corps incident' of 1924. The Guomindang government of Guangzhou, having discovered arms sent from Hong Kong to private armies organized by the chamber of commerce in Guangzhou, demanded that the chamber be disarmed, and took action that resulted in considerable casualties. The climax of political manoeuvring came in the general strike organized in Hong Kong in 1925 which dragged on into 1926. The strike had begun in reaction to the shooting of demonstrators by British policemen at Shamian and again, Guangzhou support for Hong Kong strikers was obvious. These events had come in the aftermath of another incident in Shanghai (the 'May 30th incident') in which policemen in the international settlement had shot at demonstrators, and had merged to create an anti-Western reaction across all social classes among China's urban populations. This was only toned down as the Kuomintang began its Northern Expedition and realized that the good will of the foreign powers was a necessary condition for its success.[23]

Through the 1920s, therefore, despite the prominence of the Whampoa Academy and its success in the northern expedition, the Guomindang did not control Guangdong. It did not control even very much of Guangzhou. The death of Sun Yatsen in Beijing in 1925 and the emergence of Chiang Kai-shek from the Whampoa Military Academy were events of national importance. Yet, despite the close connection with Guangzhou and the national prominence of their total suppression of the Communist Soviet founded in Guangzhou that survived for barely a week in 1927, they left little impact on Guangdong province or Guangzhou city. Instead, noticeable change came about with the rise in 1931 of strong man Chen Jitang, who succeeded in bringing about a programme of economic reform for Guangdong before he was ousted by Chiang Kai-shek. Unlike other warlords, Chen Jitang is fondly remembered by Guangdong people. He had taken charge of Guangdong as the province slid rapidly into depression, and by promoting the sugar industry and the cultivation of sugar cane in areas that had formerly been devoted to mulberry and silk, Chen created a semblance of economic vitality. Chen Jitang's regime, however, was the last time Guangdong stood up to central authority from the north. With his retirement to Hong Kong in 1936, the central government, now located in Nanjing, took charge of Guangdong.

War broke out in 1937. Guangzhou came under air attack almost immediately and was lost to Japanese troops in 1938.

25

Massive numbers of refugees appeared in Hong Kong, until Hong Kong itself came under Japanese attack and fell in 1941.[24] The war from 1941 to 1945 signalled the end of an era, for the Kuomintang government was soon to withdraw to Taiwan and the People's Republic declared in Beijing. The Chinese Communist Party, none the less, had returned to Guangdong long before that declaration. During the war, guerrilla forces under the Fourth Army of the Chinese Communist Party had been established in numerous parts of Guangdong. As in many other parts of China, the new regime established control quite rapidly in 1949.

GUANGDONG FOR THE GUANGDONG PEOPLE?

Several themes recur frequently in Chinese history and they become very apparent in any discussion on regional experiences over a long period of time. Of these themes, two stand out in the history of Guangdong. First, Chinese regional politics varies in relation to the credibility of the central government not only in the region concerned but also in the whole country. Second, the economy prospers when the country is opened to outside trade and withers when it is not.

These two themes are well borne out in the history of Guangdong. Also borne out is a less commonly discussed theme in Chinese history: that a regional sense of identity emerges not only when the region stands off from the centre, but also when the region reacts to the cultural and political inroads made by the centre. Autonomy and secession have long been contradictory themes in Chinese politics. China has been unified too long as a single country, and the Chinese people are too convinced of themselves as a nation, to entertain any idea of outright secession. Yet, some degree of autonomy in political affairs, which strengthens every time the centre fails to hold its grip on local sentiments, will remain a source of instability until the national ideology has found a place for it. In the days when Guangdong people demanded that the warlords be ousted from the province, their slogan was 'Guangdong for the Guangdong people'. Never, though, did they cease to believe that Guangdong people were also Chinese and that they should react to national politics as such. In the final analysis, local groups that struggled for power were not opposed to provincial consciousness, but then, neither did they ever put down arms because of their provincial affiliations.

Caught in short-term contests for power, warring factions had little use for ideology except for short-term alliances. The need for stability in the interest of economic development argues that the objectives of warring factions have to be subsumed under broader interests that find expression in ideological terms. Meanwhile the economy grinds on, adding to the grist in its mills skills and business acumen accumulated from the centuries of experience when Han met Arabs or Indians, Portuguese or British, where under the one country, there were not only two but many systems. As the tide of the southern seas might describe it, if it could speak, the ships, men, goods, currencies and ideas from far-off lands that surge with it onto the shores might seem to vary from time to time, but Guangdong has continued to extend into the water. Commenting on the ebb and flow of its traffic, the tide might even say, 'There goes yet another tightening of rule and its relaxation.'

NOTES

1. For background, see David Faure, 'The lineage as a cultural invention: the case of the Pearl River Delta', *Modern China*, 15, 1 (1989): 4–36; and S. T. Leong, 'The Hakka Chinese of Lingnan: ethnicity and social change in modern times', in David Pong and Edmund S. K. Fung (eds.), *Ideal and Reality, Social and Political Change in Modern China, 1860–1949*, Lanham, MD: University Press of America, 1985, pp. 287–326.
2. Edward H. Schafer, *The Vermilion Bird, T'ang Images of the South*, Berkeley: University of California Press, 1967.
3. Liu Zhiwei, 'Ming-Qing Zhujiang sanjiaozhou diqu lijiaji zhong "hu" de yanbian', (The transformation of the household in the *lijia* tax registration on the Pearl River Delta in the Ming and the Qing) *Zhongshan daxue xuebao*, 3 (1988): 64–73.

27

4. Huo Tao, *Huo Wenmin gong quanji* (The Complete Works of Huo Tao), preface of 1552, 1862 reprint, 10B/15a.

5. Huo Yuxia, *Huo Mianzhai ji* (Collected Works of Huo Yuxia) 1857, 11/75b.

6. Robert Y. Eng, 'Institutional and secondary landlordism in the Pearl River Delta, 1600–1949', *Modern China*, 12, 1 (1986): 3–37.

7. 'The family admonitions of eighth-generation ancestor the venerable Huaiting', in the *Taiyuan Huoshi zupu* (Genealogy of the Huo surname from Taiyuan), manuscript held in the Foshan Museum, unpaginated.

8. On the trade at Guangzhou, see John King Fairbank, *Trade and Diplomacy on the China Coast, the Opening of the Treaty Ports, 1842–1854*, Stanford: Stanford University Press, 1969 (first publ. 1953), pp. 39–73.

9. Cecil Clementi, *Cantonese Love-songs*, Oxford: The Clarendon Press, 1904.

10. On the politics within Guangdong in connection with the First Opium War, see James M. Polachek, *The Inner Opium War*, Cambridge: Council on East Asian Studies, Harvard University, 1992, pp. 137–75.

11. Frederic Wakeman, Jr., *Strangers at the Gate, Social Disorder in South China, 1839–1861*, Berkeley: University of California Press, 1966.

12. Polachek, *Opium War*, and F. Wakeman, *Strangers*, pp. 61–70 and 109–16.

13. Virgil Kit-yiu Ho, 'The limits of hatred: popular attitudes towards the West in Republic Canton', *East Asian History*, 2 (1991): 87–104 may be read in contrast to J. A. Turner, *Kwangtung, or Five Years in South China*, London: S. W. Partridge & Co., 1894 (reprint, Hong Kong: Oxford University Press, 1982) for an impression of Guangdong culture in the late nineteenth and early twentieth centuries.

14. Robert Y. Eng, *Economic Imperialism in China, Silk Production and Exports, 1861–1932*, Berkeley: Institute of East Asian Studies, University of California, 1986.

15. Excellent documentation on overseas Chinese investment in Guangdong may be found in Lin Jinzhi and Zhuang Weiji, *Jindai huaqiao touzi guonei qiyeshi ziliao xuanji (Guangdong juan)* (A selection of source materials on the history of overseas Chinese investment in enterprises in China in modern times, volume on Guangdong), Fuzhou: Fujian Renmin, 1989, and Michael Godley, *The Mandarin-Capitalists from Nanyang: Overseas Chinese Enterprise in the Modernization of China, 1893–1911*, Cambridge: Cambridge University Press, 1981.

16. David Faure, *The Rural Economy of Pre-liberation China, Trade Increase and Peasant Livelihood in Jiangsu and Guangdong, 1870 to 1937*, Hong Kong: Oxford University Press, 1989.

17. Jian Youwen, *Baishazi yanjiu*, Hong Kong: Jianshi mengjin shuwu, 1970 gives an account of Chen Baisha very much in the fashion he was regarded in Guangdong. An account of the relation of Guangdong

scholarship to provincial identity may be found in May-bo Ching, 'Literary, ethnic or territorial? Guangdong culture in the late Qing and the early Republic', in Tao Tao Liu and David Faure, eds., *Unity and Diversity: Local Cultures and Identities in China*, Hong Kong: Hong Kong University Press, forthcoming.

18. For a very brief note on the history of the Cantonese opera, see Bell Yung, *Cantonese Opera, Performances as Creative Process*, Cambridge: Cambridge University Press, 1989, pp. 8–10.

19. Ng Lun Ngai-ha, *Interactions of East and West, Development of Public Education in Early Hong Kong*, Hong Kong: Chinese University Press, 1984; K. C. Fok, *Lectures on Hong Kong History, Hong Kong's Role in Modern Chinese History*, Hong Kong: The Commercial Press, 1990; and Jung-fang Tsai, *Hong Kong in Chinese History, Community and Social Unrest in the British Colony, 1842–1913*, New York: Columbia University Press, 1993.

20. Edward J. M. Rhoads, *China's Republican Revolution, the Case of Kwangtung, 1895–1913*, Cambridge, Mass.: Harvard University Press, 1975.

21. Daniel H. Bays, *China Enters the Twentieth Century, Chang Chihtung and the Issues of a New Age, 1895–1909*, Ann Arbor: University of Michigan Press, 1978; Edward, Rhoads, *Revolution* pp. 91–4.

22. Useful background for this period with some discussion of the situation in Guangdong may be found in C. Martin Wilbur, *The Nationalist Revolution in China, 1923–1928*, Cambridge: Cambridge University Press, 1983.

23. Harold R. Isaacs, *The Tragedy of the Chinese Revolution*, New York: Atheneum, 1966; Fernando Galbiati, *P'eng P'ai and the Hai-lu-feng Soviet*, Stanford: Stanford University Press, 1985; Hans J. Van de Ven, *From Friend to Foe, the Founding of the Chinese Communist Party, 1920–1927*, Berkeley: University of California Press, 1991.

24. A fascinating account of the experience of rural Guangdong during the war and after may be found in Helen F. Siu, *Agents and Victims in South China, Accomplices in Rural Revolution*, New Haven: Yale University Press, 1989.

2 GOVERNMENT AND POLITICS

Elfed Roberts and Winston Ng

Guangdong province is in the forefront of change in the People's Republic of China. Not only was it among the first to undergo the major economic reforms in the drive for modernization initiated under Deng Xiaoping, but it was one of the first two provinces (Fujian was the other) to establish Special Economic Zones (SEZs) on an experimental basis. It was also in the forefront of experimentation to update the local administration in the drive for efficiency. More contentiously, many see Guangdong in the leading pack pushing for a greater degree of autonomy from the centre. The province has the fastest economic growth rate in the People's Republic of China with a gross domestic product (GDP) which doubled in the period 1980 to 1990. Indeed, many of the questions relating to China's future, and no doubt some answers, are to be found in the study of the politics of Guangdong. Within the broad framework of China's future in relation to political developments and the question of regionalism, federalism, or disintegration, Guangdong and its behaviour might provide some crucial clues to future trends.[1]

Guangdong has a marked sense of what the Chinese would call *difang zhuyi* (localism) which has contributed to the identification of loyalty to a geographical unit other than the nation-state alone.[2] Historically, and largely because of its geographical location, the province established its horizons across the sea looking to the West as well as to the imperial

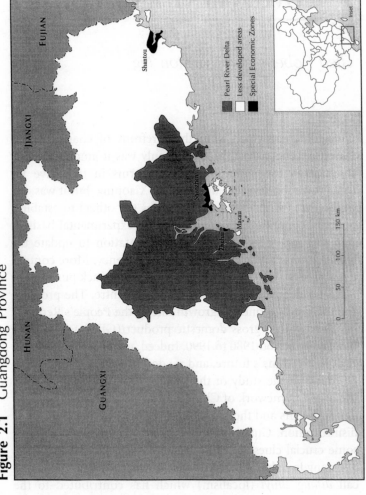

Figure 2.1 Guangdong Province

- Pearl River Delta
- Less developed areas
- Special Economic Zones

FUJIAN

JIANGXI

HUNAN

GUANGXI

Shantou

Shenzhen

Macau

Zhuhai

0   50   100   150 km

Inset

governments to the North. Linguistically it has its own language, Cantonese which is markedly different from other Chinese 'dialects' and which is far more commonly spoken than the official national language, Mandarin (Putonghua).[3]

Personal identification, although subordinate to the all-embracing Chinese nation, is sufficiently distinct and different to allow legitimate reference to the Cantonese people. Indeed, there is some truth in the Chinese proverb that 'the mountains are high and the Emperor far away' when applied to the attitude of the Guangdong people looking to their neighbours far to the north. Economically, a long tradition of trade with Asia and the West, a robust entrepreneurial spirit, and a willingness to embrace new opportunities was only briefly stifled by the establishment of the People's Republic of China in 1949. That economic dynamism was, however, among the first to emerge in the major reforms begun by the Chinese leadership in Beijing in 1978. With the acceleration of economic reforms there were to follow changes in the administrative structures, a change in the nature of accountability to the central government on matters relating to economic reform and a recognition of the need to find a new political relationship with the central authorities.

Guangdong province is in the southern part of the People's Republic of China, (approximately longitude 110E–117E and latitude 20N–25N). Moving from west to east, it has land borders with Guangxi, Hunan, Jiangxi, and Fujian provinces. To the south lies the South China Sea with Hainan province[4] situated off the south-west tip of Guangdong. Finally, Hong Kong, the British administered territory (until 1997), lies on the eastern estuary of the Pearl River. Macau, the Portuguese administered territory (until 1999), is on the western side of the same river. The national capital Beijing (Peking), is 1,887 kilometres from the provincial capital of Guangdong, Guangzhou (Canton). The total area of Guangdong is some 177,901 square kilometres, larger than England at 130,439 square kilometres. There is some 2,400 kilometres of coastline bordering on the South China Sea.

The population of the province has been increasing rapidly over the last ten years from 56,810,000 in 1982[5] to an estimated 63,489,500[6] in 1991. The population grew partly by natural increase, but more markedly by a migration of the population from both the surrounding provinces and those in the north. For example net migration increased the population by 1.25 per cent in 1978, rising to 2.14 per cent in 1991.[7] Total population density is 356.88 per square kilometre. The population is unevenly distributed however with nearly 10 per cent living in the provincial capital, Guangzhou, alone. With the rapid economic developments in the province concentrated in the lowlands of the south, on or around the Pearl River, it is hardly surprising that there has been a drift of population from the less developed areas concentrated in an inland crescent of the province which stretches north-west to north-east. Most of the population are primarily Cantonese although there are important non-Cantonese groups, the most important being the Hakka.[8]

There is little question that the Cantonese in Guangdong have had a long association with the outside world. In terms of economic activity much of the history of the province has been far more outward looking than other provinces. Seaborne trade between the Pearl River Delta area and Indochina can be traced to the fourth century, from India in the fifth and from Arabia in the sixth. Consequently, Guangzhou became, from the fourth century onwards, the most cosmopolitan and mercantile of all Chinese cities. Extensive trade with Europe came somewhat later with the arrival of the Portuguese in the sixteenth century (obtaining a lease on Macau under tribute to the Chinese in 1557), and the British in the second half of eighteenth century. Despite opposition from the Qing (Ch'ing) Dynasty (1644–1911), British interests dominated, with the consequence that China was forced to cede an area of Guangdong, namely Hong Kong Island (1842), to the colonizing power. Also, after 1842 the whole of Guangdong province was subject to increasing economic intrusion by the West under agreements forced upon a reluctant central government in Beijing. Throughout the nineteenth century, Guangdong in general, and Guangzhou in particular, remained a centre of trade with the outside world, much of which was channelled through Hong Kong.

Such intimate contact with the European powers, by now firmly established in Guangdong, led to the recognition by many in the province of the need for political change. The dynamism of the West, with its markedly differing political and economic ideas, was in stark contrast to the obvious short-comings of the late Qing dynasty. That dynamism, allied to the humiliation of the Chinese people by the colonizing powers, was to produce many local leaders agitating for radical political reform, not only for Guangdong, but for the whole of China. The ideas for reform were often championed by Cantonese who had travelled abroad, many of whom had received a Western education.[9] In particular, Sun Yatsen, the founder of the Chinese Republic, was Cantonese. Indeed, the revolution which was to topple the Qing dynasty was largely funded and originally centred in the province. The drive by the Kuomintang to unify China under its leadership (The Northern Campaign 1926–28) also began in Guangdong province.

ORIGINS OF ECONOMIC REFORM

With the victory of Mao Zedong in 1949, Guangdong was largely cut off from its traditional contact with the West. External trade with China (excepting that with the Soviet bloc), which had begun to revive following the Second World War, collapsed with the establishment of the American embargo shortly after the outbreak of the Korean War.[10] After that, increasing Party interference through a centralized bureaucracy and a vertical administrative socialist system of economic control stifled local and provincial initiatives. That combined with such disastrous policies as the nation-wide Great Leap Forward (1958–61) and the Cultural Revolution (1965–69) had a profoundly negative influence in the province.[11]

With the death of Mao Zedong on 9 September 1976, the stage was set for major reforms in the PRC that were to have profound effects upon Guangdong province. The modernization of agriculture, industry, science and technology, and defence were made official policy under the rubric of the 'Four Modernizations', and included in the Party and state constitutions on 18 August 1977 and 5 March 1978, respectively. Hua Guofeng's vision of the means to achieve economic modernization failed to reach their objectives. His ideas for reform were effectively subordinated to those of Deng Xiaoping and his moderate supporters. Guangdong was fortunate to have, as provincial party secretary from 1974, Wei Guoqing who was a close ally of Deng. Furthermore, in 1979 Xi Zhongxun and Yang Shangkun, who sided with Deng, became the leaders in Guangdong. It would be mistaken to suppose, however, that Guangdong province had a major effect upon the decision to modernize as this was primarily a central government decision.

In the same year, the central government decided to implement special policies that granted greater flexibility to two provinces in particular, namely, Guangdong and Fujian. Both were in southern China with Guangdong looking to the Hong Kong connection and Fujian facing Taiwan across the Taiwan Straits. Both also had a tradition of emigration. These emigrants still maintained links with their provinces and might have proved a rich source of investment from abroad. It was, therefore, no coincidence that these were chosen, as the policy of interior-orientated investment at the expense of the coastal regions had proved both costly and inefficient.

In 1979, Guangdong's distribution of per capita industrial output by province (percentage of national average), had fallen compared to some of China's other provinces. Dali Yang commented in his article that, 'Between 1957 and 1979 the per capita industrial output of five of the eleven coastal regions declined'. Conversely, the main beneficiaries had been many poorer regions of the western and central region provinces.[12] Growth rates, however, averaged 8.9 per cent in gross agricultural and industrial output value against an average of 9.8 per cent national growth, with the emphasis on heavy industry and agriculture at the expense of light industry. Just before the introduction of the Four Modernizations, Guangdong was ranked seventh and eighth respectively in gross domestic product and national income. In 1979 the province was to benefit increasingly from reforms, so much so that it moved up the league table to first and second places during the 1980s.[13]

The easing of controls from the central government was the first essential precondition for change. That process, tentative at first, accelerated during the period between 1979 and 1994, despite occasional attempts by the conservative faction at the centre to slow things down. Guangdong and other coastal regions were allowed to surge forward, largely at the expense of the geographical regions in the central and western provinces.

The policy of economic reform led to a major review of the administrative structures by which the province was governed. The old administrative and political structures inherited in 1978, quite simply, would not have been able to accommodate effective economic modernization. It is instructive, for a moment, to look at the areas of economic change in more detail and to analyse how these nurtured further demands for reforms, particularly in the administration of the province.

Sweeping reforms were introduced to allow for the general policy of devolving power in economic management from central government to Guangdong province. These reforms identified, in the field of management, the liberalization of production planning, technical policy, capital construction, supplies of materials, foreign trade, commodity distribution, wage levels, cultural activities, health care, and tourism.

Equally significant was the shift in the balance of investment strategies from the centre to the provinces. Financial contracting systems, including those with foreign interests, were reorganized, again giving the province a major say. The sharing of foreign exchange revenue was a matter of consultation between Beijing and the province itself, with Guangdong increasingly retaining large balances on an expanding base. General fiscal revenue for the balance of remittance to the

37

central government and retention in the province worked most markedly in favour of Guangdong.

As far as Guangdong was concerned, the relationship with the outside world was of great significance, hence the Open Door policy. Decentralization of foreign trade, with the right of local officials to conduct business, was actively encouraged. This policy, although hesitant at first, soon bore fruit. Between 1983 and 1987, the value of Guangdong's exports doubled. In 1988, overseas exports increased by a further 38 per cent.[14] That trend, despite a brief hiatus after the Tiananmen Square massacre, continued to burgeon in the 1990s. Between 1950 and 1978, and 1979 and 1988, there was an increase of 260 per cent in total exports. Detailed figures from 1991 show total exports trebling in the five years from 1985 to 1990. The period 1990 to 1991 alone showed a 30 per cent increase.[15]

In 1988, Guangdong attempted to liberalize even further, submitting a report to the central government arguing for state control over the economy to be reduced to a guiding role only. That request, in combination with the arguments between the reformists and conservatives in Beijing, was to remain unresolved in the brief period prior to the Tiananmen Incident. Li Peng and Yao Yilin, the more conservative of the leaders, wished to slow the rate of economic growth to some 6 per cent. One of Guangdong's strongest allies in central government, Zhao Ziyang, was purged. The result, albeit temporary, was a victory for the conservatives which resulted in a slow down in growth, with Guangdong having to reduce investment, and subject itself to greater macroeconomic control from Beijing.[16]

The reformists, with Deng Xiaoping at the head, reentered the fray in 1992, championing the acceleration of reforms with a growth target of at least 10 per cent. It was no coincidence that Deng chose Guangdong province to promote his policies. In January 1992, he visited Guangdong with its booming towns and the Special Economic Zones, and praised it as a model for the rest of China.[17] In the National People's Congress in the spring of 1992, Deng was triumphant[18] and Guangdong was set for even faster growth based on a high degree of economic autonomy.[19] Deng's economic policy of rapid growth was directly supported by the Guangdong authorities. Zhu Senlin made two major policy speeches in March 1992 both praising the pace of economic reform espoused by Deng.[20] Indeed, the province was quick to respond to Deng's encouragement, suggesting just how much it had felt restrained, like a race horse champing at the bit. In March 1992 a major new set of economic initiatives was announced. The Special Economic Zones, the Pearl River Delta, and areas adjacent to the Delta were told to speed up reforms and encourage even more investment from the outside world.[21]

That pace of growth, however, was not uniform throughout Guangdong. Inside the province itself, three areas can be viewed differently, namely the Special Economic Zones, the Pearl River Delta, and the crescent stretching from the northwest to the north-east. It is worthwhile paying attention to the divergencies that exist.

THE SPECIAL ECONOMIC ZONES

The Special Economic Zones (SEZs) in Guangdong are of great significance. By far the most important is Shenzhen (adjacent to Hong Kong and 327.6 square kilometres), the much smaller Zhuhai bordering Macau (121 square kilometres) and Shantou (52.6 square kilometres situated some 300 kilometres east of Hong Kong on the coast of Guangdong province). Hainan, established as an Administrative Region under Guangdong in 1981, was upgraded in 1988 to a province in its own right and therefore falls outside of this chapter.

The SEZs are an innovative administrative unit of the governmental structure of the PRC. They were established in 1980 specifically to help in the Four Modernizations, as doorways through which two-way traffic could pass between China and the outside world. The basic idea, still operative, was that foreign business, joint ventures, and the use of foreign capital, technology, and techniques could be introduced in the SEZs. This would allow for the benefits to percolate into the rest of the province and the country, without the more disruptive effects that might arise from their wholesale introduction. In this sense the SEZs were experimental workshops in new managerial, and even governmental styles.[22]

The SEZs offered all kinds of benefits to prospective investors, from which other areas were excluded. These benefits included more relaxed entry and exit regulations, business registration regulations, labour and wage regulations, land regulations, and preferential tax treatment. Significantly, SEZs controlled most, and sometimes all, of their own foreign exchange earnings, a privilege that was curtailed in 1991 to some 50 per cent.

These reforms have profoundly transformed the SEZs. Economically, Shenzhen, by far the most significant one, has outperformed even the most optimistic expectations of the early 1980s. A rather amusing new maxim in China is that 'There is nothing a Pekingese won't say, nothing a Shanghainese won't wear, nothing a Cantonese won't eat and no money a Shenzhenese won't earn'. Certainly figures seem to bear out the entrepreneurial skills present in the SEZ. Its gross domestic product has increased by an annual average rate of 50 per cent per year since 1980, reaching RMB 17.4 billion (US$3.16 billion) in 1991; exports over the same period have climbed by an annual average of 75 per cent to US$3.4 billion. Wages for an unskilled worker are some RMB 500–700 per month compared with RMB 150–200 in the Pearl River Delta.[23] In the five-year period between 1991 and 1995 the plans were for an annual GDP growth of 17 per cent and an increase in gross industrial output of 16.5 per cent. That projection was revised upwards following Deng's successful call for a 10 per cent growth in the national economy.[24]

General economic growth in Shenzhen, however, has not been without political and social costs. Corruption has undoubtedly increased in both the private and public sectors, and private and industrial rents have increased enormously. The population has grown dramatically, from 70,000 in 1978 to an estimated two million legal residents (and 500,000 illegals), thus straining the health, housing, and educational infrastructure. Inflation is eating away at the standard of living and there are disturbing signs of the growth of 'sweat shops' as well as marked differentials in levels of pay. Prostitution and vice are also areas of growing concern. In 1994 a series of accidents highlighted the problem. Illegal structures collapsed, killing those inside, safety precautions have been totally ignored, and a number of factories have been badly damaged or destroyed by fire. All these factors have led to dissatisfaction in Shenzhen that, although muted at the moment, could in the longer term alienate the government from important sectors of the governed.

NEW POLITICAL STRUCTURES

There have been attempts to design an administrative system that meets the requirements of Shenzhen, more suited to the changing circumstances. The executive is elected by the local people's congress and confirmed by the centre. The SEZ itself is under the formal authority of the State Council, and not the Guangdong provincial government. It should not be assumed, however, that the local Shenzhen officials are without a degree of power and influence.[25] They have lobbied regularly to allow greater autonomy for the SEZ and have met with considerable success. This applies not only in the strict economic sphere where power of decision-making has rapidly devolved, but also to other areas of administration. The process culminated, after intense lobbying in Beijing and opposition from Guangdong officials, in the granting of legislative powers to the Municipal People's Congress, a privilege hitherto reserved to provincial governments.[26] Examples of where Shenzhen is pressing for a different set of legislative procedures, include: stock market rulings more attuned to the West; the further easing of border controls with Hong Kong; and further restraints upon movement into the SEZ from other parts of Guangdong. Much of the pressure for change has come from the business and finance communities in Shenzhen who have transmitted their demands to the local authorities and through them to Beijing.

Most attention has been given to the Shenzhen SEZ, as it is economically the most important and has been in the vanguard of experimental change. The other two SEZs in Guangdong (Zhuhai and Shantou) tend to follow rather than lead.[27] However, there is no question that they are moving in the same direction as Shenzhen, albeit at a slower pace.[28]

Guangdong province, outside the Special Economic Zones, has also undergone a host of governmental reforms since 1978. All have been introduced in response to rapid changes taking place in the province itself. Prior to 1978 there was only one prefectural-level city, namely Guangzhou. Other areas were prefectures directly under the provincial government. Prefectures were subdivided into county, city, commune, brigade, and production team. This form of government was more attuned to the days of Mao. It was inefficient, over-centralized both at provincial and national level, and led to a lack of economic coordination between the urban and rural areas. It was also overly hierarchical and ignored the needs of horizontal and integrative planning. With the Four Modernizations demanding a more streamlined, efficient, and responsive local administration, wholesale reforms were introduced. These reforms, which took place throughout the 1980s, culminated in the major changes which took place in the 1988 reorganization.

It had long been recognized that local government in the province was overly bureaucratic, with too much control over microeconomic decision-making by both the central and provincial governments. The basic decision was to allow more freedom to the smaller units, with higher levels of government assuming more of a guiding rather than a controlling function. Administrative units were reorganized into Prefectural Level Cities (PLC).[29]

Now Guangdong province is reorganized so that all the old type prefectures (which are still to be found in many other provinces) have disappeared. The units in 1993 consisted of a total of twenty prefectural-level cities and six county level cities. There were sixty-nine counties and three autonomous counties (the latter being for the minority groups and directly controlled by the provincial government).[30] Below the county was the town administrative unit (see Figure 2.2).

The advantages of the new organizations are easily identified.

Figure 2.2 Administration Divisions of Guangdong

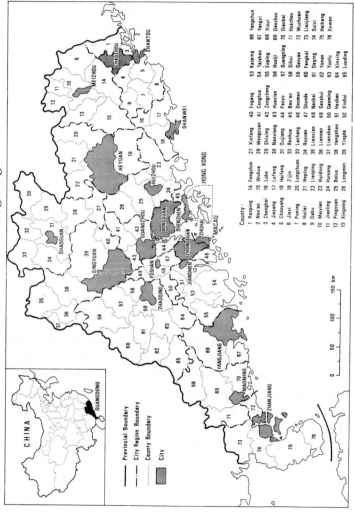

County :

1 Raoping	14 Fengshun	27 Xinfeng	40 Fogang	53 Kaiping	66 Yangchun
2 Nan'ao	15 Wuhua	28 Wengyuan	41 Conghua	54 Taishan	67 Yangxi
3 Chenghai	16 Luhe	29 Shixing	42 Zengcheng	55 Enping	68 Xinyi
4 Jieyang	17 Lufeng	30 Nanxiong	43 Huaxian	56 Huaiji	69 Gaozhou
5 Chaoyang	18 Haifeng	31 Dujiang	44 Panyu	57 Guangning	70 Dianbai
6 Jiexi	19 Zijin	32 Renhua	45 Bao'an	58 Sihui	71 Huazhou
7 Puning	20 Longchuan	33 Lechang	46 Deumen	59 Gaoyao	72 Wuchuan
8 Huilai	21 Heping	34 Ruyuan	47 Shunde	60 Fengkai	73 Lianjiang
9 Dabu	22 Lianping	35 Lianxian	48 Nanhai	61 Deqing	74 Suixi
10 Meixian	23 Huidong	36 Lianman	49 Sanshui	62 Yunan	75 Haikang
11 Jiaoling	24 Huiyang	37 Lianshan	50 Gaoming	63 Yunfu	76 Xuwen
12 Pingyuan	25 Boluo	38 Yangshan	51 Heshan	64 Xinxing	
13 Xingning	26 Longmen	39 Yingde	52 Xinhui	65 Luoding	

Source: Guangdong: Survey of a Province Undergoing Rapid Change, eds. Y. M. Yeung and David K. Y. Chu, Hong Kong: Chinese University Press, 1994. Reprinted by permission.

Divisions are simpler and conform more clearly to economic function. The distinctions between the rural and urban areas are less marked, thus allowing for a smoother transition as industrialization and commercialization progress in the province. Horizontal linkages encourage cooperation, bureaucratic delay is reduced, and information flows are more efficient. Integrated planning is improved and points of decision-making more easily identifiable.

The broader provisions for local government were outlined in the 1982 State Constitution of the People's Republic of China. In Article 30 the administrative framework was divided into three layers of government, namely provinces, autonomous regions, and municipalities directly under the central government. Under the provinces (of which Guangdong is one) have been added autonomous prefectures (PLCs in the case of Guangdong), counties, autonomous counties, and cities. Counties are then subdivided into townships, nationality townships, and towns (see Figure 2.3).[31]

In each unit there are provisions for congresses and local government organs. The local congresses above the level of county are allowed to establish standing committees. From the county level upwards there is the indirect method of election. That is, deputies to the Guangdong People's Congress, directly under the control of the central government and county people's congresses, are elected to office by the people's congresses at the next lowest level. At the county level and below there are direct elections by constituencies to office.[32] The terms of office are now five years, except the lower echelons which are limited to three years.[33]

The lower congressional levels are designed specifically to consider local economic and cultural development and the development of public services. At county level and above the function of the legislative branch is to examine and approve plans for economic and social developments, the budgets of their respective administrative areas, and the plans for their implementation. There is also the clear provision that at provincial level, the making of local regulations is permitted but that they must not contradict those of the national constitu-

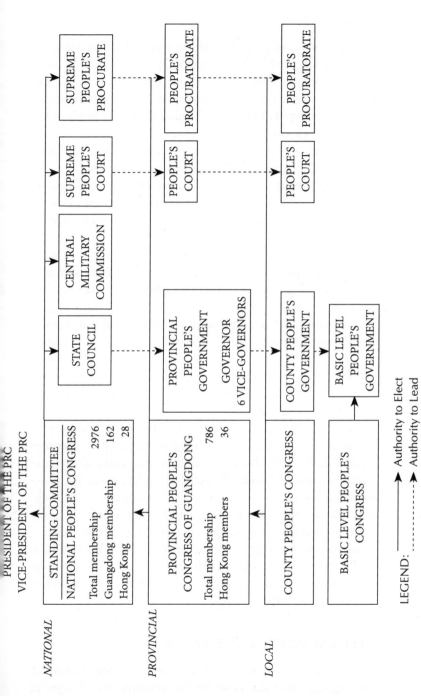

PRESIDENT OF THE PRC
VICE-PRESIDENT OF THE PRC

NATIONAL

| STANDING COMMITTEE |
| NATIONAL PEOPLE'S CONGRESS |

Total membership	2976
Guangdong membership	162
Hong Kong	28

STATE COUNCIL

CENTRAL MILITARY COMMISSION

SUPREME PEOPLE'S COURT

SUPREME PEOPLE'S PROCURATE

PROVINCIAL

| PROVINCIAL PEOPLE'S CONGRESS OF GUANGDONG |
| Total membership | 786 |
| Hong Kong members | 36 |

PROVINCIAL PEOPLE'S GOVERNMENT
GOVERNOR
6 VICE-GOVERNORS

PEOPLE'S COURT

PEOPLE'S PROCURATORATE

LOCAL

COUNTY PEOPLE'S CONGRESS

COUNTY PEOPLE'S GOVERNMENT

PEOPLE'S COURT

PEOPLE'S PROCURATORATE

BASIC LEVEL PEOPLE'S CONGRESS

BASIC LEVEL PEOPLE'S GOVERNMENT

LEGEND: ──────▶ Authority to Elect
         - - - - -▶ Authority to Lead

Note: With thanks to John P. Burns, University of Hong Kong.

tion and must, when proposed, be reported to the Standing Committee of the National People's Congress for the record.[34] Furthermore, the requisite local people's congresses elect and have the power to recall governors and deputy governors, or mayors and deputy mayors, or heads and deputy heads of the lower congressional echelons.[35]

The executive organs of government at the provincial level are outlined in Articles 105–111 of the State Constitution. The chief executives are, in descending administrative units, governor, mayors, county heads, and town heads. They are designed for the administration of 'work concerning the economy, education, science, culture, public health, physical culture, urban and rural development, finance, civil affairs, public security, nationalities affairs, judicial administration, supervision and family planning in their respective administrative areas. They issue decisions and orders, appoint, remove and train administrative functionaries, appraise their work or punish them'.[36] In the event of a conflict, the next and higher level of government has the power to impose its decisions. On a hierarchical ladder the line of authority moves up, at least constitutionally, inexorably to the highest level at central government, namely the State Council.

There is little question that the trend in both local government, in the congresses in Guangdong (partly as a consequence of the administrative reforms mentioned above, and partly because of rapidly changing attitudes within the province) has led to an increasing level of autonomy at all levels, even though there are variations in the degree of autonomy enjoyed by different geographical areas. It would be inappropriate to assume that provincial government takes kindly to undue interference, particularly in those areas it sees as of local concern, from the central government organs, as will be discussed later in this chapter.

REFORM WITHIN THE PARTY

Unlike the major administrative reforms undertaken in Guangdong since the Four Modernizations, the changes in the Party structure have been much more modest. Power still flows in a downward direction from the centre to the province. Each upper level ensures that the lower levels observe the directives sent to them (see Figure 2.4). Statements emanating from top political cadres looking to increase the legitimacy of the Party by introducing structural reforms have not been associated with any real action. Granted that first some changes were made in 1984 when a degree of decentralization of personnel management of the Party took place, with the Central Committee and other Party Committees enjoying *nomenklatura* authority over only one level down the hierarchy.[37] (This meant that Beijing directly controlled the appointment of key provincial posts in Guangdong, but not appointments at the lower levels.) Second, attempts were made to professionalize the cadres, establish clearer objectives for the Party in the new economic environment, and improve the efficiency of the Commission for Discipline Inspection at provincial and county level.[38] Third, Li Peng, in a speech on 1 October 1991, stated that 'China is implementing the reform of the economic and political structure. We think that the reform of the economic structure must be commensurate with that of the political system'.

Nevertheless, the political reforms enacted were in the administrative sphere outside the party rather than in the Party itself. This position was reinforced by the experience of the Soviet Union, where the collapse of party authority led, in the eyes of the Chinese hierarchy, to the chaos that has ensued. That experience was made even more urgent by the Tiananmen Incident, which brought to a screeching halt any tentative moves to reduce Party dominance. The nightmare of loss of control by the central Party still haunts the leaders. Any attempts to allow other parties to gain effective influence, any loss of authority by the Party, any deviation from ideological directives, were given short shrift. Even three years after Tiananmen, the amendment to the Party Constitution adopted on 18 October 1992 made allowance for the economic changes by entering the theory of 'building socialism with Chinese characteristics', but not for the devolution of Party power.

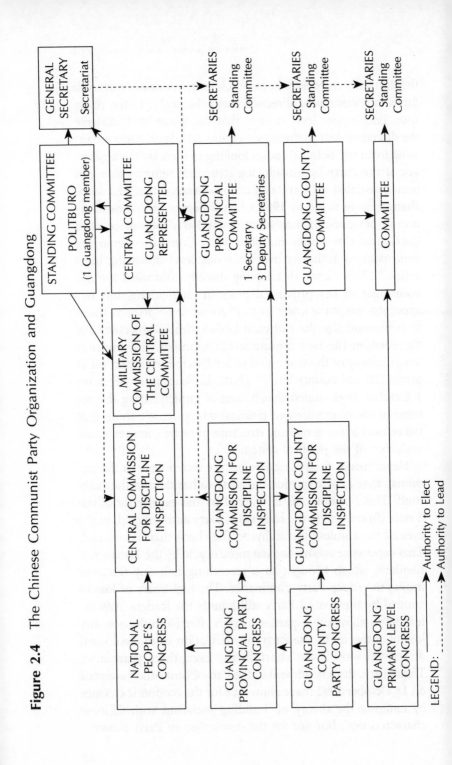

Figure 2.4 The Chinese Communist Party Organization and Guangdong

Indeed, no reference to reorganization, Party moderniza- tion, or devolution of power was considered. Instead the emphasis at the Thirteenth CPC Central Committee, from which the constitutional amendment emerged, was on im- provement of work style within the prevailing structure, eco- nomic modernization, and the elimination of corruption. To achieve this, all Party members, Communist Youth League members, workers, peasants, intellectuals, cadres, people's armed forces, democratic parties, mass organizations, and even patriots with no political affiliations were called to strengthen ties with the masses. Indeed, far from looking towards a more relaxed style of control, the theme was Party discipline, strict observance of the Party line, and adherence to the 'four car- dinal principles'.[39]

How successful the Party has been in imposing its author- ity in Guangdong is another matter. As will be seen later, the provincial Party members at the centre are not without influ- ence. They have combined with other provincial leaders at the central level to press their case for lessening of economic constraints. They allied with Deng to continue the economic reforms when they were under question from factions at the higher levels of the Party. Equally significantly, the local Party members worked with other areas of government in the in- terests of Guangdong province, forming an alliance with the emerging economic-reform pressure groups. Whilst rarely challenging the ideological dictates from Beijing, in many circumstances their application of those directives has been lukewarm when not really approved. (Good examples are the response to the Tiananmen Incident and the treatment of dissidents, and the same could be said of the central decision in 1989 to slow down growth rates in the province and the attempts by Guangdong to circumvent such moves.)

With many of the cadres at all levels coming from Guang- dong itself, and given the reformist nature of those cadres, it is hardly surprising that they have sometimes circumvented in action that which they approve of in words. Equally signifi- cant are the signs, certainly in the lower echelons of Party cadres, of a marked lack of enthusiasm for political work and indoctrination. Despite attempts to inculcate dedication and to impose discipline, success seems to be limited at the grass roots. Finally, as will be seen, the masses in the province are more concerned with more pressing matters than Party ideology and control.

DIVISIONS OF WEALTH

Wealth and progress are not equally distributed within Guangdong. It is, therefore, useful to divide Guangdong province (excluding the SEZs) into two broad areas namely the Pearl River Delta and the outer, more mountainous areas stretching from the north-west to the north-east (see Figure 2.1).

The Pearl (Zhujiang) River Delta has long been the most affluent area in the province. It has, of course, the navigable river that divides Hong Kong and Macau, a position close to the South China Sea, a relatively good communications system, and, as indicated earlier, long historical and cultural connections with the outside world. The early choice of Guangdong province as an area with special privileges, outlined in the Four Modernizations programme, benefited the area enormously. Its early start gave the impetus for further benefits in February 1985 when the cities and counties of the inner delta were amalgamated into a larger unit termed the Pearl River Delta Economic Development Zone. Within that zone were four cities, Foshan, Jiangmen, Zhongshan, and Dongguan, and twelve counties. In October 1984, Guangzhou was made into an open coastal city and it was granted provincial-level economic power in 1984. In both cases it built upon special tax and other incentives to attract further outside investment and export opportunities.

The results of administrative changes discussed earlier, combined with the growing economic and fiscal privileges, resulted in the phenomenal economic growth of the coastal zones. From lagging behind the Shenzhen SEZ they quickly took on a momentum of their own, not least because, unlike the SEZs, more local officials tended to hold positions of power (the SEZs were much more under the control of central appointees). These local officials had an unofficial network of mutual connections, not only in the province, but increasingly with Hong Kong and even in Beijing. This situation helped to cut down bureaucratic delay, attracted investment, facilitated cooperation between horizontal and vertical decision-making groups, and fostered continual contact between the government officials and private business.

The more hilly and mountainous area which forms 60 per cent of the land area of Guangdong, with just over 40 per cent of the population, is on the other hand, markedly different from the Pearl River Delta.[40] Partly because of its geomorphology, less developed communications, and its distance from the major centres of economic development, it has not shown the same degree of resilience as other regions in the province (it still only produces 21 per cent of the total income). The preponderance of the poor is found here in the rural areas. If regional distribution of rural per capita net income in 1990 is taken as a guide, the situation becomes clearer. In the Inner Delta Area the rural income is 1,360 yuan compared to 845 yuan in the hilly and mountainous regions.[41] Even more marked is the disparity between income in the cities or economic zones where the figure is 2,535 yuan.[42] In simple terms the average person working the land in the mountainous region is earning only 35 per cent of the counterpart in the cities to the south, and the gap is widening.[43]

The provincial and central governments have attempted to address the problems which income disparity brings in its train. Various and complicated plans to rationalize the system, get rid of the premodernization communalization, and encourage different agricultural and forestry programmes were largely unsuccessful. The incomes of the residents in this area continued to show a relative decline. Improvements were patchy at the best when compared to the richer areas of the lowlands. Although there was some attempt to transfer some resources into the area from the region of rapid growth in the province (mostly under pressure from central government) through various policy initiatives, success was limited.[44]

Far more significant has been the movement of people from

these areas to the south in search of work. The developing lowland economic areas have proven to be a magnet for those from the mountainous regions looking for employment.[45] As the immigrants are generally less educated than the lowlanders there has been a tendency for them to find work as semi-skilled and unskilled workers in the booming construction industry of the inner crescent.

The migration has had major political effects in both the lowland and highland areas. In the former case many un-skilled workers have flooded south, exacerbating unemploy-ment and the shortage of housing, education, and hospital provision, and contributing to a surge in crime, vagrancy, prostitution, and corruption.[46] At the same time inflation has risen to dangerous levels with all its associated problems.[47] The old economic system and many political controls im-posed prior to 1978 have largely disappeared with the new entrepreneurs showing little if no interest in ideological mat-ters. The workers are more concerned with wages and mater-ial goods. The result is a culture generally apathetic to major political interference from outside the province.[48] Control by the old Party cadres, the work unit (*danwei*), and the old bosses in the state factories has withered away, or is in the process of doing so, at an ever faster rate. The ability of the party to regulate information flows is diminishing.[49] The Party also has to convince the growing non-agricultural population that unrestrained growth, and the widening gap between agri-cultural and industrial workers, are threatening economic and political instability. In the mountainous areas depopulation caused by the movement of young people from the villages, and the loss of authority of both village elders and Party cadres in the old agricultural system, are taking their toll.

What can be seen is the development of new patterns of identification, more divorced from the old ideas of loyalty to ideology, the traditional Communist Party orthodoxy, or, as will be seen later, of subordination to central government when it is seen to conflict with provincial or local interests. Pressure groups, not least those centred on the emergence of new entre-preneurs, are increasingly involved with the promotion of policies that benefit their sectoral concerns. Access to decision-making provincial centres and officials, both Party and bureaucratic, increases daily, and the arguments presented are increasingly listened to sympathetically. These pressure groups are impatient with red tape, anxious to promote rapid economic expansion, and annoyed by perceived unwarranted interference from the central decision-making nexus in Beijing. This trend is likely to become more vocal, albeit in restricted circles, should Beijing embark on a course perceived as detrimental to rapid economic growth in the province.

LABOUR UNREST

There are also signs that the workers in Guangdong province in general, and in Shenzhen in particular, are looking beyond the Party, to assume a more positive role in the protection of their interests. The traditional function of the All-China Federation of Trade Unions (ACFTU) has always been that of control and interest representation on behalf of the central government and Party. Increasingly the more reform-minded union officials hope to see it develop as an organization to support workers. In 1988, a new charter was accepted by the Communist Party. It clearly stated that in the case of a strike the role of the union was to represent the interests of the workers in negotiations with the employer and not merely to act as spokesmen for the government. In the rapidly developing areas of Guangdong and the SEZs, where private enterprise is paramount, there is no question that the workers are looking to improve wages and in particular working conditions. It appears, therefore, as if two seemingly contradictory trends are emerging.

On the one hand, many factory workers' wages are rising rapidly, allowing for savings. Workers increasingly exercise the right to move from factory to factory in pursuit of higher wages, and have rising expectations for the future. Those employed in the non-state sector have sacrificed the social security safeguards of the old state factory system and many seem to prefer the greater freedom of working in the new enterprises.

On the other hand, many factories in the rapidly developing areas are notorious for their poor safety record and lack of social security provision. The poor working conditions, as indicated previously, were clearly demonstrated by the disastrous fire in a Shenzhen toy factory in 1993. The total death toll in industrial accidents for the whole of China was 11,600 in the period January to August 1993, an increase of 112.9 per cent over the same period in the previous year.[50] Although figures for the province are difficult to locate, there is little question that the rise is even more pronounced in Guangdong. Local agitation in response to the increasing casualty rate prompted the All-China Federation of Trade Unions to send down investigatory teams to inspect safety conditions.[51] With inflation eroding salaries, poor working conditions and a declining safety record, agitation on behalf of the workers is increasing. Whether the ACFTU will provide the leadership, and will be identified by the workers as the legitimate negotiator on their behalf in the future, or whether other informal actors, who are fairly insignificant at the moment, will appear, remains to be seen. At present an estimated 70 per cent of all joint venture factories are not unionized at all. On the wider front a large number of *ad hoc* labour organizations have cropped up in Guangdong. Despite Chen Ji's (the ACFTU deputy policy research director) protestations that, 'China has no independent unions at all and doesn't need them', it would appear that some activity is taking place. Han Dongfan,[52] a Hong Kong-based mainland labour activist calling for the reform of trade union laws, stated that if, 'workers don't have their own unions to represent them, who else can truly represent their interests?'. Unless the ACFTU can rid itself of its quiescence, and unless the conditions in the factories are markedly improved, there is fertile ground for the growth and expression of independent labour organizations in the future.

The New Interest Groups

Other groups in Guangdong are also gaining influence, if not to the same extent as those mentioned above. Some peasants are suffering from a fall in income, compared with their counterparts in the urban areas, and are increasingly concerned about unfair taxes, rising land prices, inflation and corrupt officials. Most of these are concentrated in the less developed parts of the province. They increasingly have become disillusioned with the central government, which they feel has ignored their interests, and the provincial and subprovincial authorities, who they feel have ceased to provide services. Other peasants in the rapidly developing south, however, are making large profits out of the sale of land for housing and industrial complexes. The latter category has little to complain about and tends to side with the provincial authorities in the push for economic growth.

In the field of education, the autonomy granted to academics has led them to set up alternative proposals for the governance and economic and social development of the province. It is instructive that in 1987 thirty full-time scholars left their academic positions in the liberal arts faculties around the province to form 'Guangdong Soft Science Co.', an independent think-tank primarily involved in social and economic analysis for foreign and domestic companies.[53] Just one year later, Zheng Yanchao, a high-ranking academic in the Guangdong Academy of Social Sciences, openly advocated China's need to break with traditional Marxist thinking, arguing that new ideas were needed, to enhance the nation's production forces.[54]

Religious organizations, mostly Roman Catholic and Protestant, are proliferating in Guangdong province and actively offer a contrasting set of loyalties to those offered by the Communist Party.[55] The local authorities have waxed and waned in their attitude towards these non-approved religious organizations. Since 1978, the authorities have been more tolerant of the growth of 'house churches' but have occasionally cracked down on religious activity. In 1983, one of the most famous Christians in Guangdong, Lin Xiangao (known as 'Pastor Lamb' in the West) had his church temporarily closed down, but was then allowed to reopen. In 1988, the Religious Affairs Department of the Guangdong Provincial Government issued a document named the 'Stipulations on Administrative Management of Religious Activity Venues in Guangdong Province'. It required religious organizations to register with the government to conduct religious services. These new regulations were employed, after the Tiananmen Incident, to try to rein in Pastor Lamb, who had refused to register. In October 1993, there were further raids on unregistered places of worship, although it was thought that these were in response to the failure of China to host the Olympic games. Despite these crackdowns, however, there is very little question that the officials in Guangdong are far more tolerant of the Christian denominations than most other provinces. There are few, if any, underground churches and the degree of persecution is far below that of many other provinces.

Another potential pressure group, namely the Student Pro-democracy Movement, found it more advantageous to work with, rather than against, the local provincial government. When, for instance, the central government in Beijing was suppressing the pro-democracy movement with undue force, in Guangdong there was no bloodshed and no martial law. Those few dissidents who were arrested were released without charge or have suffered short sentences. This was despite tens of thousands taking to the streets after the declaration of martial law in Beijing on 20 May 1989 and despite the barricading of provincial government buildings for twelve days. In fact, the mood of cooperation between the provincial officials and the students led to agreements to demonstrate only in the evening so as not to disrupt traffic. Most significantly the slogan chanted by the students was very much in tune with the position, before and since, of provincial officials, 'Stabilize Guangdong, protect the fruits of reform'.[56] After the crackdown in Beijing, and the concomitant pressure upon government authorities to detain dissidents fleeing from the capital city, it is thought that Guangdong officials acted slowly enough for 300 or so to be smuggled out of the country.

If emerging interest groups are more inclined to work with, rather than against, the provincial authorities, many in the provincial government are also sympathetic towards these groups. The authorities support those who are helping economic growth, are tolerant of those who do not challenge stability, and turn, for the most part, a blind eye on dissident groups as long as they do not go too far.

THE HONG KONG INFLUENCE

Economic and political change is also increasingly being encouraged by forces outside of the province, not least from Hong Kong. The symbiotic relationship between the Territory and Guangdong has intensified almost by the day. Guangdong has received huge investment from the Territory which accounts for over 80 per cent of the total from overseas. High wage rates and land costs in Hong Kong have led to a huge movement of Hong Kong's manufacturing base across the border, where an estimated three to four million workers are employed by Hong Kong business in outward processing-related activities. By 1990, Hong Kong–China trade had exceeded HK$400 billion which amounts to a fifty-fold increase since the introduction of the Four Modernizations. The close family, clan, and business links with the inhabitants of Hong Kong, who are overwhelmingly Cantonese, has seen the cross-border train movements of persons into Guangdong province increase from some 2.2 million per annum in 1977 to 38 million persons per annum in 1992. Some 60,000 Hong Kong businessmen are now in Guangdong province, bringing with them the values, beliefs, and practices of the Territory which, in turn, are more in tune with Western commercial and financial norms. The Hong Kong dollar circulates freely in Shenzhen and Guangzhou and is often the currency of choice for business and investment.

Contacts between the authorities in Hong Kong and Guangdong are proliferating at a dizzy rate. In 1978, cooperation between the authorities was largely restricted to formal and sporadic contact on such questions as the return of illegal immigrants, and the supply of foodstuffs and water supply. The last twelve years have seen regular contact and communication in a host of areas. This was caused initially, and primarily, by the growth in economic relations and furthered by the reductions in border controls and the concomitant need to encourage functional cooperation. Such functional areas as Immigration control, Customs control, corruption and law and order are subjects of regular discussion. Delegations from parallel organizations regularly make cross-border visits for briefings and joint planning in such diverse areas as the development of the stock market in Shenzhen, harmonization of business, financial, and legal practices, comparative public administrative practices, and academic exchanges.[57] At the same time, many businessmen from Guangdong province are working in Hong Kong either in their own businesses or on secondment to firms in the Territory.

When Hong Kong reverts to the sovereignty of the People's Republic of China, it will be administered as a Special Administrative Region (SAR) of the PRC under the overall control of the Standing Committee of the National People's Congress.[58] The SAR is guaranteed a high degree of autonomy, with very distinctive institutional structures, a major divergence in the roles of the judicial branch, and in the criminal and civil law, active and competing political parties and interest groups, and the provision for freedoms formally denied to other provinces and regions in the PRC. Within the constitutional framework Hong Kong is clearly different and separate from any administrative or formal political structure in Guangdong.

Nevertheless, in reality, the two systems are moving towards markedly increasing functional cooperation in major areas of mutual concern. There are no indications that the process will be reversed in the future, as the economic links are becoming indissoluble. As Guangdong's growth relies in no small part on the goodwill and continued involvement of Hong Kong, so does the future prosperity of the Territory lie firmly with the PRC in general, and Guangdong province and the Pearl River Delta in particular. The border, for economic purposes, is permeable to a degree never dreamt of as recently as twelve years ago when the SEZ was in its infancy. Administrative practices and procedures, although different, are beginning to show signs of limited convergence, which with the practices in Hong Kong provides a general example that counterparts in Guangdong are inclined to follow.

Another increasingly interesting political development is the fostering of relationships between the provinces. The centripetal forces encouraged in the premodernization period have been undermined by a degree of centrifugalism between the fast growing provinces on the one hand and the laggards on the other. The forces of disunity and unity have a strong precedent in the history of China, a hardly surprising fact given the sheer size of the country and its geographical, cultural, and linguistic diversity. Such differences between regions and provinces have been further marked by the encouragement of interprovincial cooperation in the economic field and between the provincial governments. As vertical control was undermined in the administrative reforms within Guangdong province, to be replaced by horizontal cooperation, so did the same general trend manifest itself in interprovincial relationships. Major reforms were introduced which either lessened or abandoned central monopoly over agricultural goods, commodities, procurement and sale of industrial products, and the wholesale commercial system. Trade between Guangdong and the provinces burgeoned at the provincial, city, and county levels, and largely independent of central government.

Some indication of this can be seen from the following. In 1988 a 'Liaison Centre for Central and Southern China Economic and Technical Cooperation' was set up in Guangzhou. By 1985, Guangdong had already signed 2,409 agreements and contracts on economic and technological cooperation with twenty provinces, cities, and autonomous regions, with a total investment of RMB 2.273 billion. That figure had increased to 6,781 agreements with other provinces and units by 1986.[59] In this way Guangdong helped to guarantee its supplies of food and raw materials. It set up joint enterprises and production and sale bases in other provinces, along with marketing and maintenance networks for Guangdong's own enterprises. Inward investment from other provinces into Guangdong also took place so that other provinces could establish export channels, market their products in Guang-dong, and establish their own marketing and maintenance networks.[60]

CONFLICT OR CO-OPERATION

The result has been a mixed blessing. The poorer provinces have increasingly felt that Guangdong and the coastal region are sucking in resources at their expense. At the same time, the gross value of industrial output (GVIO) has shown increasing disparity between the regions. If China is divided into three broad regions, namely the coastal region, central region, and western region, the share of GVIO is 61.2 per cent, 26.55 per cent, and 12.55 per cent, respectively.[61]

In the poorer regions, which are marginalized and disadvantaged, a degree of annoyance is expressed by the local governments and keenly felt by the population at large. Intense competition for raw materials has led to friction between the richer coastal areas, and Guangdong in particular, and the central and western regions who are the suppliers and who want higher prices. This has resulted in an outbreak of protectionism and the non-delivery of raw materials to the richer regions of the south despite the agreement to do so. In fact, it was admitted by one official that 'The current wave of protectionism is the worst in the last 40 years'.[62]

The disparities have led the poorer regions to seek greater investment in their infrastructures by the central government. They have asked to set up Special Economic Zones of their own and have attempted to bargain with the richer provinces for higher prices and greater investment. This, as we shall see, has had a major impact upon the unfolding relationships between central government and Guangdong province.[63]

At the same time, mutual interest has led to a major surge in cooperation, although within a competitive framework, between the richer coastal areas. These areas have perceived the need to safeguard their interests against any unwanted incursions from central government.[64] Whereas the local units are clearly specified as subordinate to the central authority in the

Constitution,[65] there is nevertheless provision for 'giving full play to the initiatives and enthusiasm of the local authorities'.[66]

It follows that, in the formal sense, central government can overrule legislation by the local units, impose decisions upon them, and negate any polices felt to be inappropriate. National policies decided at the centre are applicable to all the local units and they must abide by them. Since the introduction of the Four Modernizations, however, there is clear evidence that the rapidly modernizing provinces have increased their informal power of decision-making, particularly in the economic sphere, at the expense of the centre. There is, therefore, a clear mismatch between the informal powers of the local units and the formal constitutional relationship, leaving a grey area which the local units have been quick to exploit.

Such exploitation has taken various forms. One is taking advantage of the support afforded by Deng's modernization drive, thus legitimizing greater autonomy. Deng, in his attempts to outflank the conservatives, actively sought and procured the support of Guangdong, Shenzhen, and Shanghai officials, thus strengthening both Deng's position and their own. The power of the provinces was even further strengthened by their increasing representation in the highest organs of decision-making. Xie Fei, the Guangdong Party leader joined the Politburo in 1992, along with the CCP provincial secretaries Chen Xitong (Beijing), Jiang Chunyun (Shandong), and Wu Bangguo (Shanghai Municipality). At the level of Central Committee, two of the Guangdong CCP deputy secretaries and the governor of Guangdong were full members and two vice-governors were alternative members. Similar numbers were to be found in the other coastal provinces.

Within the province reform-oriented leaders have been appointed, increasingly from among local cadres. Both the First Party Secretary Lin Ruo and the Governor Ye Xuanping, appointed in 1985, were from Guangdong province. This trend of local appointments was repeated after 1989, when despite the reshuffles caused by Li Peng, both Xie Fei, a local cadre and Zhu Senlin, the former mayor of Guangzhou, were appointed as First Party Secretary and Provincial Governor.[67]

The push for greater autonomy by Guangdong and the emphasis on localization of government and cadres has not, as some observers have suggested, been in the direction of overt rejection of the central government's overall authority. On the question of ideological policy, the provinces have been, at least vocally, supportive of the centre. Such administrative reforms as have been introduced by the provinces have been approved by Beijing. The relationship between the party and the state apparatus is still hierarchical *vis-à-vis* the provincial level, although weakened. It is clear that central government control at the lower levels of provincial government is reduced. Recently, new financial and tax reforms introduced in January 1994 have attempted to take from the rich provinces and distribute to the poorer, so necessary if the central government is to keep credible central control. These reforms were accepted, albeit grudgingly, by Guangdong province.[68] Anti-corruption drives, law and order campaigns, and anti-Western cultural drives thought up at the centre are given lip-service support, although in practice such support is often lukewarm at best. (Even here, however, the mayor of Guangzhou, Li Ziliu, argued that speculation and profiteering were necessary under certain conditions.)[69] Any attempt to impose major ideological initiatives that might hamper economic growth would probably meet little approval by provincial officials, as the ability of the central party hierarchy to initiate and sustain mass mobilization campaigns is no longer present.

What is taking place, therefore, is most likely a resetting of the relationships between Guangdong province (and indeed the other rich provinces) and the central government. A relationship where power is decreasingly brokered from the centre, but sufficient deference is paid from the local unit for the system to continue to operate. This process is likely to continue since economic modernization is at the heart of government policy. Whether some kind of federal system with a more explicit division of power enshrined in a constitutional framework is likely to evolve is a subject of intense debate. Such a legal development would go a long way to recognizing the emerging *de facto* powers of Guangdong, and other provinces, and to reducing the current uncertainties and frictions.

What is almost certain is that Guangdong in particular, and the rapidly developing coastal states in general, are not looking towards the break up of the sovereign state. Evidence for such a preference is simply not present. There is a large difference between a powerful regional identity, opposed to undue interference from the centre, and a full-blown attempt to break away from Beijing. Despite the stresses and strains in the central–provincial relationship, a partnership still exists. That partnership is changing in so far as the previously junior partner is demanding greater consultation and freedom to operate, but it is still a partnership.

THE LIMITS OF AUTONOMY

There is little question that the whole of the People's Republic of China is engaged in a bold experiment of reform. Within the general framework of that reform, Guangdong is one of the leading provinces. It held much of the initiative throughout the 1980s and does not look as if it will lose it in the 1990s. Indeed, with the return of Hong Kong to the PRC, investment continuing to flood into the province, and the obvious overall success of both the economy and the administrative reforms, the situation looks promising.

Positive attempts are being made, albeit slowly, to come to terms with the changing political environment, both within the province and in its relationship with central government. Local elites, both political and economic are emerging, who, while not challenging the overall authority of the centre, have increased their power base both in the province and in Beijing. There is no question that pressing social problems will express themselves as the economy continues to expand. New forces, divorced from overt Party identification, are apparently growing in strength, and will probably continue to do so in the future. They will be highly critical of any attempts to divert growth in the province by the imposition of a clampdown from central government. Other pressure groups will

63

press for more rights such as the rights of workers and the rights to greater religious freedoms.

The provincial government has responded with a degree of tolerance not often shown in other parts of China. Attempts by the central government to stamp down too hard on these groups could well lead to social disturbances, a fact recognized by the authorities in Guangdong. Whereas the provincial government may recognize the need to help poorer provinces, where unrest is more evident, it will do so reluctantly if it leads to unwelcome levels of taxation or the bleeding away of resources. The possible contradiction between the perceived national needs and those of Guangdong mean that the national government has to find a compromise position. Push Guangdong and the other rapidly modernizing provinces too hard and there may be outright opposition. Refrain from attempting to relocate resources and the poorer provinces, starved of funds and support, could explode.

Whatever the relationship between region and centre, one thing is certain. There is considerable agreement between the provincial government, the administration, and the vast majority of the population of Guangdong, that market-oriented policies should continue to evolve. The marked success of Guangdong since the Four Modernizations has led government officials to predict Guangdong's inclusion among Asia's 'little dragons'. There seems little reason to dispute that claim.

NOTES

1. For an interesting article on this question see: Maria Hsia Chang, 'China's Future: Regionalism, Federation, or Disintegration', *Studies in Comparative Communism*, 25, 3 (1992).
2. Chang, *Studies*, 211–212.
3. Though there is some dispute as to whether Cantonese is a language or a dialect, what is certain is that Cantonese is certainly a language in that when spoken it is unintelligible to Mandarin (Putonghua) speakers. In the written form, however, there is little difference.
4. Hainan, once a part of Guangdong province, was made an Administrative Region in 1981 and a full-fledged province in 1988.
5. Gerald Chen (ed.), *China Handbook*, Hong Kong: *Ta Kung Pao*, 1982, p. 2.

6. Statistical Bureau of Guangdong Province, *Statistical Yearbook of Guangdong 1992*, Beijing: China Statistical Information and Consultancy Center, 1992, p. 67, Figure 1.2.
7. Statistical Bureau of Guangdong Province, *Statistical Yearbook of Guangdong 1992*, Beijing: China Statistical Information and Consultancy Center, 1992, p. 131, Figure 3.1. I am also indebted to Dr Ronald Skeldon who has provided me with the following figures on migration from other provinces to Guangdong from 1985 to 1990. (As these are official figures, they are probably an underestimate.)

Guangxi	432,000
Hunan	239,000
Sichuan	168,000
Fujian	61,000
Jiangxi	59,000

8. There are a number of minority groups in Guangdong province. *The People's Republic of China Yearbook* for 1991/1992 includes the Zhuang, the She, and the Yao. There are also a large number of other smaller minority groups. The total minority population was estimated in 1992 at 145,200, who were mostly to be found in the mountainous region. When Hainan was still part of Guangdong, the minority population was much higher. The Hakka are not considered a minority group.
9. In particular Liang Qichao and K'ang Yuwei led the demands for reform and change within the Qing Dynasty. Both were from Guangdong and were heavily influenced by Western ideas, by the continued humiliation of the Chinese by the West, and by the refusal of the Qing dynasty to recognize the need for major reforms in the political system.
10. An indication of the breakdown in trade can be seen in the figures for exports from Hong Kong to China. The figure fell from US$221 million in 1951 to less than US$11 million in 1970. Yun Wing Sung, *The China–Hong Kong Connection: The Key to China's Open Door Policy*, Hong Kong: Cambridge University Press, 1991, p. 20.
11. For the Cultural Revolution and its effects on Guangdong province, see Ezra Vogel, *One Step Ahead In China: Guangdong under Reform*, Cambridge, Mass.: Harvard University Press, 1989, Chapter 1.
12. Dali Yang, 'Patterns of China's Regional Development Strategy', *The China Quarterly*, 122 (1990): 238–39. The figures he quotes in the distribution of per capita industrial output in Guangdong are as follows.

Distribution of Per Capita Industrial Output by Province
(Percentage of average)

Year	1957	1965	1974	1979
Guangdong	84	94	85	79

13. Wang Xue Ming, 'Guangdong: Economic Growth and Structural Changes in the 1980s', in *Guangdong: 'Open Door' Economic Develop-*

ment Strategy, Hong Kong: Centre of Asian Studies, The University of Hong Kong, and Institute of Developing Economies, Tokyo, 1992, p. 18.

14. For details of Guangdong's economic relationships, see Zhu Jia Jian, 'Guangdong's Economic Relationships with Central Government And With Other Provinces/Municipalities', in Toyojiro Maruya (ed.), *Guangdong: 'Open Door' Economic Development Strategy*, Hong Kong: Centre of Asian Studies, The University of Hong Kong, and Institute of Developing Economics, Tokyo, 1992, pp. 98–125.

15. *Statistical Yearbook of Guangdong 1992*, p. 58.

16. In terms of investment in the infrastructure and technical innovation, the figures show a major decline. In the first quarter of 1989 there was a 33 per cent increase over the last quarter of 1988. By the fourth quarter of 1989 there was a 8.8 per cent drop from the previous quarter. Despite this, however, the level of investment began to recover in late 1990 before Deng's triumph in 1992. *See Statistical Yearbook of Guangdong 1992*, pp. 12–13.

17. On 13 April 1993, Jiang Zemin reaffirmed the policy of Deng, as he stated on the fifth anniversary of the establishment of Hainan province: '[The idea of the] SEZ is postulated by Deng himself, he created and designed this new project, and made it to be of central importance to our country. SEZ is the "window" of our "open door policy". We must search for the appropriate way to enforce our reforms. It [the SEZ system] can provide valuable experience to enrich and to re-establish our Chinese style of Socialism.' *People's Daily (Overseas)* (14 April 1993): 1 (translation).

18. After Deng's visit, it was claimed that Guangdong had started the 'second liberation of new thinking'. *People's Daily (Overseas)* (24 March 1993): 1 (translation).

19. After Deng's visit, Guangdong set a new economic goal which aimed to catch up with the economic development of the 'Four Little Dragons' within twenty years. *Hong Kong Economic Journal Daily* (14 January 1993) (translation).

20. 'Guangdong Zhu Senlin Comments in Hong Kong Zhongguo Tongxun She' (in Chinese) in FBIS-CHI-92-056, 23 March 1992, and Zhu Senlin reviews Guangdong development, *Beijing Xinhua* (in English). Reported in FBIS-CHI-92-058, 25 March 1992.

21. 'Guangdong Makes Arrangement to Open Up More Boldly to Outside World'. *Renmin Ribao Overseas Edition* (in Chinese). FBIS-CHI-92-045, 6 March 1992.

22. Shenzhen was the first place in China granted legislative powers to the Municipal People's Congress. A former mayor of Shenzhen pointed out that the development of a market economy, legal system, and democratic institutions would have to progress at the same pace. He believed that Shenzhen should be *the* experimental workshop in creating a legal

structure for a market-oriented system. *People's Daily (Overseas)* (23 March 1993): 4 (translation).

23. *Far Eastern Economic Review* (13 May 1992): 26. For detailed figures relating to Shenzhen SEZ, see *Shenzhen Special Economic Zone Yearbook 1992*, Hong Kong: Guangdong People's Publisher, 1992.

24. The Director of Shenzhen Trade Development Council even stated that Shenzhen could, as in the case of Guangdong, reach the status of the Asian 'Four Little Dragons' within twenty years. *United Daily News*, 20 January 1993. (translation).

25. The top officials in Shenzhen's government in 1992 were to be found in Shenzhen Municipal People's Government. Names and details are in the *Shenzhen Special Economic Zone Yearbook 1992*.

26. The detailed composition and membership of the Shenzhen Municipal People's Congress can be found in *Shenzhen Special Economic Zone Yearbook 1992*.

27. Shantou was created as the first experimental city to carry out business administrative reform under the auspices of the Industry and Commerce Bureau in 1993. *Ta Kung Pao* (20 January 1993): 4 (translation).

28. As a matter of fact, Shantou's economy was very strong in 1992. The total foreign investment in that year equalled the sum of the past 13 years, increasing by 50% over 1991. *Ta Kung Pao* (1 February 1993): 5 (translation).

29. Vogel, *One Step Ahead*, pp. 119–20. The author refers to these new units as Metropolitan Regions so as not to confuse them with the old Prefectures. The authors have used more literal translation which refers to these units as Prefectural Level Cities. They should *not* be confused with the old Prefectures as they are very different.

30. *Hand Book of the Administrative Division of the People's Republic of China*, Beijing: China Map Publisher, 1993, p. 52 (in Chinese).

31. The Constitution of the People's Republic of China. (Adopted on 4 December 1982 by the Fifth National People's Congress of the People's Republic of China at its fifteenth session.) *People's Republic of China Yearbook 1991–1992*, Beijing: PRC Yearbook Limited, 1993.

32. Ibid., Article 97.

33. Although the three-year term of office was under review in 1993.

34. The Constitution of the People's Republic of China, Articles 98–100.

35. Ibid., Article 101.

36. Ibid., Article 107.

37. For the *nomenklatura* system, see John Burns, 'China's Nomenclatura system', *Problems of Communism*, 36 (1987): 86–9.

38. The functions of the CCP Central Commission for Discipline are set out in Chapter 8 of the Constitution of the Communist Party of China. Its main function is to maintain authority and conformity with party directives. More recently it has been used in the Party's anti-corruption campaigns.

39. The 'four cardinal principles' are: supporting the socialist road; proletarian dictatorship; supporting the leadership of the Chinese Communist Party; and Marxist–Leninism and Mao Zedong Thought. Deng Xiaoping officially proposed the principles in December 1980 during the CPC CC working meeting. Xie Qingfui, ed., *Dangdai Zhongguo Zhengzhi*, Shenyang: Liaoning Renmin Chubanshe, 1991, pp. 69–71.
40. *Statistical Yearbook of Guangdong 1992*, p. 101.
41. Wen Simei and Zhang Yue Hue, 'Rural Economic Development and Social Changes in Guangdong Province', in *Guangdong: 'Open Door' Economic Development Strategy*, p. 69. For detailed county figures, see *Statistical Yearbook of Guangdong 1992*.
42. *Statistical Yearbook of Guangdong 1992*, p. 101.
43. Attempts have been made to improve the situation in the mountainous areas. In 1992 local governments in these areas were given permission to attract overseas investment. See 'Mountain Areas in Guangdong vie for Foreign Investment' in *Window* (2 October 1992): 28.
44. As reported by *People's Daily (Overseas)*, however, it was hailed as a great success in alleviating poverty in Guangdong's mountainous areas in 1992. It was reported that the number of people not having enough to eat was reduced from 250,000 to 200,000. The number of people in relative poverty was reduced from three million to two million. *People's Daily (Overseas)* (6 February 1993): 6 (translation).
45. Guangdong was the first province to reform the labour allocation system, thus allowing enterprises greater freedom to recruit labour in different regions of the province. This new policy helped to integrate the segregated labour market inherited from the old centralized labour-allocation system. At the same time, the labour force was granted freedom to choose employment within the province. Nevertheless, this policy further intensified the trend of labour migration. *People's Daily (Overseas)* (13 February 1993): 5 (translation).
46. There have been major attempts to control the influx of rural labourers from outside the province. Since February 1993 potential immigrants from other provinces have been limited. In 1993 the number was fixed at 150,000. Guangdong has also set up labour offices in the provinces of Sichuan, Hunan, Jiangxi, Henan, Hubei, Guizhou, Yunnan, and Guangxi provinces. *China Daily* (30 December 1993). It is questionable, however, whether this has been successfully applied, as anybody who has been to the railway stations in Guangzhou will attest.

   Regarding social factors, a public opinion survey in Guangdong conducted in 1992 indicated that while 66.4 per cent of respondents were satisfied with economic indicators, over 50 per cent were dissatisfied with such problems as public order and security, public transport, and the environment. *Ta Kung Pao*, (in Chinese) 20 January 1993.
47. Inflation in Guangzhou alone was running at a reported 24 per cent in the period January–October 1993. Despite admitting that this was a

major problem the vice mayor of the city, Chen Kaizhi reaffirmed the policy of rapid economic growth. *South China Morning Post* (12 October 1993).

48. See 'Two Faces of Reform', *Far Eastern Economic Review* (8 April 1993): 15–18.

49. On the question of control over information, large areas of Southern Guangdong are tuned into Hong Kong channels. Also Star Satellite Television has made large inroads into the province. Recently Wang Feng, the Chinese Minister of Radio, Film and Television, decided to control receivership of satellite television by Chinese citizens on the grounds that, 'Such control is beneficial to the cultivation of patriotism among our citizens, safeguarding the superior tradition of the Chinese race, promoting socialist civilization and maintaining social stability'. It will be interesting to observe whether this decision will have much effect. *South China Morning Post* (16 October 1993).

50. *Beijing Review* (27 December–2 January 1994).

51. In November 1993, a disastrous fire at the Zhili Handicraft factory in Shenzhen's Kuai Tong district led the Guangdong Authority to introduce new worker safety regulations. In June 1994, an illegally constructed toy factory collapsed, killing eleven people and injuring another twenty-seven. Such events suggest that safety regulations are disregarded by entrepreneurs and not enforced by the relevant authorities. For an interesting article on this problem, see *Far Eastern Economic Review* (16 June 1994): 32–6.

52. Han Dongfan, aged 31, a dissident active in the events of June 1989, was expelled from China in 1993 on his return from medical treatment in the United States. He has been in the fore-front of the movement attempting to create independent trade unions and has actively criticized any recognition of the ACFTU by overseas Western trade unions.

53. *Beijing Review* (14–20 December 1987).

54. *Kyodo*, 17 August, 1988 in FBIS-CHI-88-160. p. 21.

55. Regarding the growth of Christianity in the People's Republic of China, see Jinang Zhimin and Xu Zugen, 'The rise of Christianity in China', *Liaowang*, 5 (17 February 1989).

56. *Far Eastern Economic Review* (8 April 1993): 8. It would be a mistake, however, to assume that the authorities have a more liberal attitude towards crime and ill-defined forms of anti-social activity. In fact, it is estimated that up to 250,000 people in Guangdong are in some form of correctional institute. In addition, the limitations on dissent, although liberal by Chinese standards, would seem harsh by Western yardsticks.

57. In terms of cooperation between the mainland and Hong Kong, indicators clearly point out the closer relationships. In the first six months of 1993, six Policy Branches and 38 Departments in Hong Kong made a total of 166 official visits to their counterparts in China. Over the

same period, 130 Chinese groups involving nearly 1,000 officials came to Hong Kong. Areas discussed included banking supervision, infrastructural planning, policing, customs, ICAC contacts, and staff exchanges. See *Address by the Governor The Right Honourable Christopher Patten at the opening session of the 1993/94 Session of the Legislative Council*, 6 October 1993. Official Record of Proceedings, Hong Kong Legislative Council, 1993. Sections 141–2.

58. For provisions of the Basic Law, see *The Basic Law of the Hong Kong Special Administrative Region of the People's Republic of China*, Consultative Committee for the Basic Law of the Hong Kong Special Administrative Region of the People's Republic of China, April 1990. For specific reference to the interpretation of the Basic Law and the final adjudication of the Basic Law and the SAR, see Article 158.

59. Zhu Jia Jian, 'Guangdong's Economic Relationships with Central Government and with other Provinces/Municipalities', p. 120.

60. Ibid., pp. 122–3.

61. Dali Yang, 'Patterns of China's Regional Development Strategy', p. 251.

62. Maria Hsia Chang, 'China's Future: Regionalism, Federation, or Disintegration', p. 221.

63. Ibid., this article is extremely useful for a macro analysis of the strains in the regional discrepancies in the People's Republic of China.

64. The coastal region is made up of the following provinces: Liaoning, Beijing, Tianjin, Hebei, Shandong, Jiangsu, Shanghai, Zhejiang, Fujian, Guangdong, and Guangxi.

65. 'The People's Republic of China is a unitary multinational state. . . .'. *The Constitution of the People's Republic of China* (Adopted 4 December 1982), Preamble.

66. Ibid., Article 3.

67. See Peter Tsan-yin Cheung, 'The Evolving Relations between the Center and Guangdong in the Reform Era', in Jia Hao and Lin Zhimin (eds.), *Changing Central–Local Relations in China, Reform and State Capacity*, Westview: Boulder Co., 1994. pp. 207–37.

68. Interview with Premier Li Peng, *China Daily* (3 January 1994).

69. Peter Tsan-yin Cheung, 'Evolving Relations'.

3 GEOGRAPHY AND NATURAL RESOURCES

Richard Louis Edmonds

Guangdong's geography possesses good possibilities for economic development. Its subtropical and tropical climate combined with high levels of precipitation and adequate soils has given the province a strong base for agriculture. Its coastal location, relative adequacy of mineral resources, and interaction with Hong Kong, Macau, and overseas Chinese communities has facilitated the growth of industry and the formation of an outward looking entrepreneurial mentality. The concentration of population, agriculture, and industry, however, has been along the accessible lowland coastal plains, whereas the mountainous interior has remained relatively backward. The Open Door policy implemented since 1978 has reinforced the coastal orientation, making Guangdong an example of China's current regional economic development pattern: rapid accumulation of wealth along the coast with an interior which is far poorer.

CLIMATE AND GEOMORPHOLOGY

Guangdong's warm climate is a product of monsoonal wind patterns and latitude. In the summer, winds blow off the Pacific Ocean creating a warm moist environment favourable for agriculture. The annual average temperature in the province varies from about 19 ˚C in the north to 24 ˚C on the

Figure 3.1 Guangdong's Geography

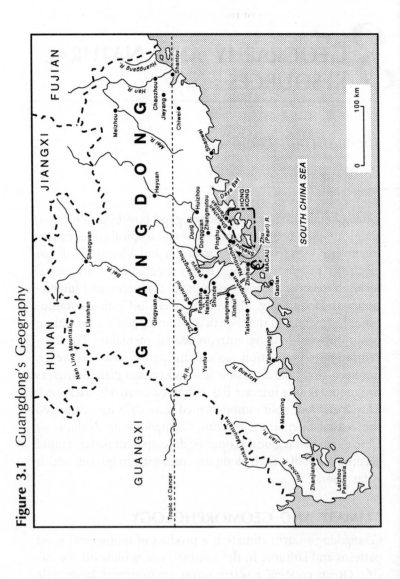

Leizhou Peninsula in the far south.[1] For all practical purposes the southern half of the province (the area south of the Tropic of Cancer) has no monthly average temperature below 10 °C and the northern half of the province has only two months of what can be considered winter. Frost periods vary from two months in the far north to virtually none along the southern coast. These conditions mean that triple cropping is possible virtually anywhere in Guangdong.

In general, levels of precipitation average between 1,400 and 2,100 millimetres per annum and are good for intensive agriculture (see Figure 3.2). There is considerable regional, seasonal, and annual variation, however, dictated largely by the strength of upper air-stream flows.[2] The rainy season starts in February or March in the northern mountains and about a month later in the central and southern areas. The dry season also comes earlier in the north, beginning in September. While rain is not as seasonally concentrated as on the North China Plain, over 40 per cent of the annual precipitation normally comes during the summer months.

Typhoons are a major cause of the preponderance of summer rainfall. The typhoon season runs from May to October with almost one typhoon hitting the province per month on average. This makes Guangdong one of the provinces most seriously affected by typhoons in terms of both frequency and intensity. A typhoon can account for a considerable amount of the annual precipitation, with sometimes over 300 millimetres falling in one day. The number of typhoons reaching Guangdong can vary from two to ten in a year.

As Table 3.1 shows, warm, moist conditions generally coincide with the period of high insolation from May to October with the lowest insolation occurring in February and March. These insolation peaks and troughs do not correspond to the high (June) and low (December) positions of the sun but are a result of solar position combined with levels of cloud cover. These high levels of insolation are particularly advantageous for agricultural development, and are one reason why Guangdong farmers are able to undertake triple cropping.

Guangdong's climate is also modified by the Nan Ling

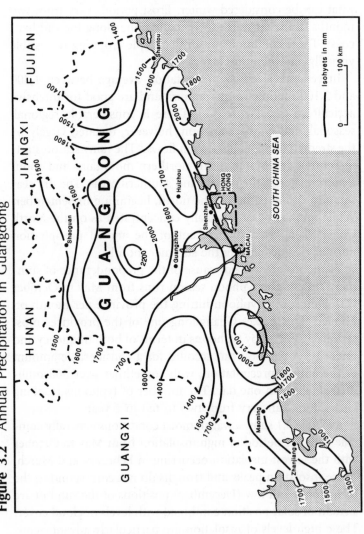

Figure 3.2 Annual Precipitation in Guangdong

Table 3.1 Insolation (kilocalories per square centimetre) and Temperature (degrees centigrade) for Selected Locations

	Shaoguan	Guangzhou	Shantou	Zhongshan
Annual total insolation	111.6	106.7	122.2	112.6
February total insolation	5.5	5.9	7.2	6.0
July total insolation	14.5	11.8	13.9	12.6
Total insolation for days with temperature greater than or equal to 10°C	97	102	119	106
Annual mean temperature	20.3°	21.8°	21.3°	21.8°
February mean temperature	11.5°	14.4°	13.8°	14.5°
July mean temperature	29.1°	28.4°	28.2°	28.4°

Sources: Wu Yuwen et al., eds. *Guangdong Sheng Jingji Dili* (Economic geography of Guangdong province), Beijing: Xinhua Chubanshe, 1985, p. 20. Zhang Tao, ed. *Guangdong Sheng Guotu Ziyuan* (Land resources of Guangdong province), Guangzhou: Guangdong Sheng Guotuting, 1986, pp. 53, 55.

mountains which stretch east–west for about 1,000 kilometres along the northern boundary with Hunan and Jiangxi provinces. The Nan Ling are composed largely of sandstone, quartz, and granite. These mountains block the entry of cold winter winds into the province.[3] Historically the Nan Ling range has also inhibited the movement of people, thus encouraging the development of distinct subcultures in Guangdong.

In contrast to the Nan Ling, the north-western boundary between Guangdong and neighbouring Guangxi is less distinctly delimited. Although the Yunkai Mountains act as a partial divide, the Xi River tributaries flow down from Guangxi in an uninterrupted fashion. As the names Guangdong ('Guang east') and Guangxi ('Guang west') imply, these two provinces were traditionally seen as a set and were administered jointly in the past. However, Guangxi is relatively higher in elevation with a very short coastline and therefore, in many ways has been an economic and cultural hinterland of Guangdong.[4]

To the south of the Nan Ling much of Guangdong is hilly. Mountains and hills occupy close to two-thirds of Guangdong's total area. Four rivers: the Mei River (the upper course of the Han River), the Dong (or East) River, the Bei (or North) River, and the Xi (or West) River dissect the province into four large segments. These rivers have very limited use for navigation and the rugged sloping nature of the hilly terrain of the north has made large scale organization of agriculture difficult, with small, dispersed fields the norm.[5] In general the higher land is of poor fertility with the better agricultural areas generally found along the valleys of the larger rivers.

Tablelands, which account for less than one-seventh of the province's total area, are concentrated in the west along the Leizhou Peninsula and in the Maoming area, but can also be found along the coast in parts of east and central Guangdong as well as in basins and valleys. In general these tablelands are rolling plains composed of quaternary reddish soils and quaternary deposits,[6] although they often contain terrace steps. The greatest problem with development of Guangdong's tablelands is their lack of water, since the high permeability of the soils means that there are usually few streams on the surface. Infertile and acidic soils as well as soil erosion have complicated attempts at agriculture. In spite of their agricultural limitations, Guangdong's tablelands are easily accessible and often densely populated.

In contrast, the lowland plains are the most agriculturally productive part of Guangdong, containing 37 per cent of the cultivated land but less than one-quarter of the total land area. The major plains are the Zhu (Pearl) River Delta and the Chaozhou–Shantou Plain.

The fertile Zhu River Delta is the largest plain in subtropical China (11,000 square kilometres) and is the core of human activity in Guangdong. The Zhu River is formed from three major tributaries: the Dong, Bei, and Xi Rivers. These three tributaries form a delta rather than a river as the Zhu splits into numerous tributaries and branches right at the point of convergence of the Bei and Xi Rivers. The considerable erosion upstream has led to the rapid deposit of silt in the delta. As silt is deposited, the streams change course, creating new islands or merging former islets. Seaward growth in places has been as much as 170 metres per annum.[7] The implications of the creation of new land for agricultural and urban expansion along the coast have been tremendous, facilitating centuries of agricultural expansion, and allowing cities to undertake coastal reclamation with ease. Moreover, the river branches throughout the delta have facilitated transport.

The Chaozhou-Shantou Plain in eastern Guangdong was formed by deposition of silt from four small rivers: the Huanggang, the Han, the Rong, and the Lian. This plain is only about one-ninth the size of the Zhu River Delta and has been fully exploited in agricultural terms with a very high cropping index, making it one of the most productive farming areas in China. Other lowland plains worthy of mention include the Moyang River Plain, the Jian River Plain, and the lowlands of the Leizhou Peninsula in the western part of the province. Although relatively small in size, their population densities are amongst the highest in western Guangdong, with the city of Zhanjiang constituting the major economic node. For the province as a whole, it can be said that while climate, soils, and flat terrain with good water courses for transport will favour further economic growth along the coast, the interior of the province remains more difficult to develop.

Land, Water Resources, and Vegetation

Land

With the exception of the extreme south of the Leizhou Peninsula where andesite (a basic, light grey, volcanic igneous rock) is the predominant parent material, most of Guangdong's soils are derived from acidic rock and granitic material. The natural soils of the province are predominantly iron and aluminium rich laterites and other reddish soils with thin organic layers on the surface with some saline and swampy soils found locally. In many places, the soils have been modified by agricultural use with the resulting soil type due as much to crops grown and cultivation techniques as to parent material. Long periods of intensive cultivation and recent industrialization have reinforced the acidic nature of Guangdong's soils.[8] In general, levels of calcium, sodium, magnesium, and potassium are low whereas iron and aluminium are high. In particular, the lack of potassium along with leached red soils are not good for agriculture, although the iron and aluminium could be useful for metallurgy. Those paddies found on lowland alluvium generally have the highest fertility.

Guangdong's per capita arable land ratio is about one-half of the Chinese national average. Although some doubt can be cast upon the accuracy of the arable land and household registration statistics, agricultural population densities are highest in the east, particularly the Chaozhou-Shantou Plain (Shantou, Chaozhou, Jieyang, Meizhou, and Shanwei) and in the Jian River Plain (Maoming) (Table 3.2). In general the flatter and more urbanized Zhu River Delta has lower levels of agricultural population per cultivated area than the east, although Shenzhen, Heyuan, and Zhaoqing all have more than 2,000 agricultural persons per square kilometre of cultivated land. Most of the lowlands in the province have been put into paddy. There is, however, still a limited amount of land available for dry field cultivation (wheat, corn, peanuts, beans, and tubers) in the northern and western parts of the province and, with the exception of high mountain peaks, other land in the north can be exploited through forestry and other activities.

However, the ratio of people to total land area in Guangdong is greater than the national average and pressure is mounting. Land continues to be lost to development, industrial growth, and water reservoir construction as well as to house building, with 1992 showing a serious imbalance between new agricultural land expansion and loss of existing cultivated area (Table 3.3). The Guangdong government now carries out inspections to see that land is being used according to its zoned use. While in 1991 558 hectares were found to be in violation of zoning regulations and dealt with accordingly, this only represents a small part of the problem. In addition, the cultivated-land statistics in Table 3.3 hide the fact that it is generally good quality agricultural land that is being taken out of cultivation and poorer quality land which is being added.

Water

With such high levels of precipitation and a geologic structure that favours percolation, Guangdong is blessed with good surface water and ground water resources, especially by comparison with northern and north-western China. In addition to considerable local precipitation, the province also benefits from fluvial transport of water from neighbouring areas, especially Guangxi. There are thirty-three rivers in the province with catchment areas larger than 1,000 square kilometres.[9] All of the rivers in Guangdong ultimately flow into the Pacific Ocean. These conditions make Guangdong one of the best provinces, if not the best, in terms of per capita water resources. In general, per capita levels of water availability are highest in the mountainous north around Shaoguan and lowest in the east around Shantou. However, availability of surface water is about 80 per cent concentrated in the moister six months of the year. With cropping virtually continuous throughout the year, drought conditions can easily occur during the winter months as happened during 1991.

Ground water replenishment is particularly good in the Leizhou Peninsula of the south and in the northern Guangdong karst region. It was estimated that the Leizhou Peninsula can supply 5.05 million cubic metres of ground water a day from within about 300 metres of the surface and the north Guangdong karst region can supply 14.39 million cubic metres per day.[10] However, development of ground water resources has proven difficult and in certain parts of the province people are still short of drinking water. In eastern Guangdong there are a considerable number of warm springs. Most of these

Table 3.2 Land and Population Characteristics for the Twenty Prefectural-level Municipalities (*shi*) of Guangdong, 1992[a]

	Total population (thousands)	Surface area (sq. km.)	Cultivated area (sq. km.)	Population per sq. km. surface area	Population per sq. km. cultivated area	Agricult. pop. per sq. km. cultivated area
Guangzhou	6,122.1	7,434.4	1,518.0	823.5	4,033.0	1,688.8
Shenzhen	2,609.0[b]	2,020.0[b]	103.4	1,291.6	25,232.1	2,207.9
Zhuhai	549.7	1,630.0[c]	361.2	337.2	1,521.9	769.7
Shantou	3,819.4	2,019.5	216.5	1,891.3	17,641.6	12,884.5
Shaoguan	2,872.7	18,360.0	1,323.6	156.5	2,170.4	1,476.6
Heyuan	2,832.9	15,620.0	1,123.7	181.4	2,521.0	2,385.1
Meizhou	4,430.9	16,194.0	1,397.1	273.6	3,171.5	2,682.5
Huizhou	2,393.3	11,157.7	1,372.9	214.5	1,743.2	1,267.1
Chaozhou	2,232.8	3,080.9	452.1	724.7	4,938.7	3,822.0
Shanwei	2,349.7	5,247.0	746.0	447.8	3,149.8	2,457.2
Dongguan	1,360.6	2,640.0	563.4	515.4	2,415.0	1,834.5

Zhongshan	1,192.5	1,680.0	526.1	709.8	2,266.8	1,677.8
Jiangmen	3,614.8	9,443.4	1,802.1	382.8	2,005.9	1,433.4
Foshan	2,911.5	3,624.6	1,018.5	803.3	5,136.4	1,820.4
Yangjiang	2,319.9	7,615.0	1,152.3	304.7	2,013.3	1,597.4
Zhanjiang	5,678.1	12,404.8	3,424.1	457.7	1,658.3	1,328.7
Maoming	5,428.7	11,230.3	1,733.8	483.4	3,131.1	2,705.6
Zhaoqing	5,687.5	21,134.2	2,304.7	269.1	2,467.8	2,084.4
Qingyuan	3,477.76	20,155.0	1,825.6	172.5	1,904.9	1,587.8
Jieyang	4,564.9	5,392.5	1,033.6	846.5	4,416.5	3,796.0
Total	64,641.7	177,901.0	24,031.9	363.4	2,689.8	2,006.7

Sources: Guangdong Sheng Tongjiu, ed. Guangdong Tongji Nianjian 1993 (Statistical Yearbook of Guangdong 1993), Beijing: Zhongguo Tongji Chubanshe, 1993, pp. 61, 154, 174, 467–70. Wu, Guangdong Sheng Jingji Dili, pp. 4–12.
a Population statistics are based upon household registration statistics and therefore, are likely to underestimate the actual population. Cultivated area statistics have also come under criticism for under-representing actual totals. Provincial statistics in this table are based upon Guangdong totals found in the Statistical Yearbook and vary from the sum of local figures due to different sources or to rounding.
b Statistics from Shenzhen Tongji Nianjian 1993, p. 35. Population figure includes 'temporary population' which is excluded in the official provincial yearbook figure.
c Excludes water surface.

Table 3.3 Changes in Cultivated Land Area in Guangdong (in hectares)

	1985	1989	1990	1991	1992
Total addition	*11,746*	*25,280*	*21,513*	*17,140*	*12,947*
New land	3,520	9,500	10,693	8,733	6,080
Polder	—	493	2,060	2,260	927
Abandoned and other land	—	15,287	8,760	7,827	5,940
Land taken out of cultivation	*79,313.3*	*19,587*	*17,267*	*33,427*	*89,107*
Total change	−67,567	+5,693	+4,246	−16,287	−76,160

Source: *Guangdong Tongji Nianjian 1991*, p. 127; *1993*, p. 154.

ground water sources have a low mineral content although some along the coast are alkaline.

With over 3,360 kilometres of coast line and over 1,000 islands, the development of marine-based economic activities is quite favourable. There are about 150 natural harbours suitable for fishing fleet bases with approximately 120,000 hectares of ocean available for pisciculture. Needless to say, ocean shipping has played and will continue to play a vital role in Guangdong's economic development. We shall take a closer look at port development when we discuss transportation.

Vegetation

Due to Guangdong's warm climate, the vegetation varieties are quite abundant with over 5,000 species of natural flora. A considerable number of these are useful as medicines, oils, starches, fibres, and raw materials for the petrochemical industry.

Forests are a valuable if not plentiful resource. Types of forest include: subtropical evergreen-broadleaf natural forests found mainly in the north, subtropical monsoon secondary forests widely distributed in central latitudes, and tropical evergreen monsoon forests on the Leizhou Peninsula. In addition to these, tropical savanna is found on the tablelands of the Leizhou Peninsula where the primary tropical monsoon forest has been removed by humans. There are also mangroves and other salt-tolerant plants growing in the coastal areas. Natural forests, however, are now mostly confined to areas where accessibility is poor.

Perhaps the most widely distributed tree type is the evergreen conifer, the Chinese red pine (*Pinus massoniana* D. Don ex. Lamb., in Chinese *maweisong*), which can be found throughout the province except for the extreme south of the Leizhou Peninsula. The second most common tree is the China fir (*Cunninghamia lanceolata* (Lamb.) Hook, in Chinese *shan*), which grows in hilly and mountainous areas. Of the foreign-introduced varieties, eucalyptus (*Eucalyptus* spp., in Chinese *an*) and the horsetail casuarina (*Casuarina equisetifolia* L., in Chinese *mumahuang*) are the most common and found predominantly in coastal locations.[11] There is virtually no natural grassland in the province, but instead areas which have been deforested and are now covered with secondary vegetation. The quality of this grassland is poor, with only about 10 per cent of the province's total area suitable for grassland herding. With so much of western China more appropriate for herding than agriculture, it is irrational to advocate expansion of grassland herding in Guangdong. There is, however, some possibility for herding and forestry expansion in combination which could increase strained local meat supplies.

Recent afforestation efforts began with shelterbelt planting on the Leizhou Peninsula in 1954. However, the overall trend, at least up to the late 1980s, has been for reduction in forest area.[12] During the late 1970s, *Eucalyptus* spp. and pine were planted, followed by broad-leaved mixed trees in certain areas. This activity, combined with a subsequent shift to a mixture of tropical crop trees and fruit trees in the 1980s, shows that recovery can be quick if properly managed. Indeed, plantation forestry is gaining in importance. In 1986 the most recent version of the national Forestry Law was ratified and the law was implemented in Guangdong, at least in name.[13] Currently the Zhu River Delta is being reforested as part of the Great

Plains Project, an attempt to increase the area of forest on some of China's major plains.

In 1992 Guangdong officially was 53.7 per cent covered by forests with at least a 30 per cent canopy closure. In that year Guangdong produced 21.4 per cent of China's pine resin and 11.1 per cent of the national output of rubber, making it a significant supplier of these raw materials. Although tea is not technically a forest crop, Guangdong also produced 5.1 per cent of China's tea output on 3.9 per cent of the national area devoted to tea planting. Other important tree crops in the province include banana (over 60 per cent of 1992 national production), oranges (33 per cent), longan (*Euphoria longana*), lychee, carambola, papaya, and pomello. Many of these fruits find ready export markets in Hong Kong and Macau.

Forestry in Guangdong, however, faces several problems. The forest stock of 230 million cubic metres is only just under 2.5 per cent of the national total. Clearly this is inadequate for the needs of local industry and Guangdong is already a net importer of timber. Neglected pine saplings are susceptible to pest infestation, especially the pine caterpillar (*Dendrolimus* spp., in Chinese *songmaochong*). These insects have already caused serious drops in the production of pine resin.[14] Moreover, the possibility of new pest and disease threats is always around the corner. For instance, pine wilt disease caused by the pinewood nematode (*Bursaphelenchus xylophilus*) is endemic in Hong Kong with Chinese red pine the principal species infected.[15] The major problem for the future of forestry in Guangdong will be balancing timber forests, protection forests and so-called 'economic tree crops', while demand for forest products and forested land increases. More efficient management initiated during the 1980s has made a start but as forestry is a long-term matter, it will require vigilance and increased efficiencies in coming years.

Guangdong has always been famous for its wild fauna. It is said that there are 500 species of birds, over 100 species of mammals, and eighty of amphibians. Rapid economic growth, however, coupled with a growing Cantonese appetite for wildlife restaurants, is reducing the number of fauna and the future for wild animals is not particularly good. It has been noted that fish stocks at the mouth of the Zhu River and in the nearby shallow seas are being depleted.[16] With depletion of fish stocks all along the China coast now a recognized fact, there should be considerable potential for importing fish to Guangdong.

THE MINERAL BASE

Estimates of reserves have been made for over eighty-five minerals in Guangdong, and mining is being carried out in more than 1,400 locations in the province (see Figure 3.3). There are known to be large quantities of non-ferrous metals. The Nan Ling range contains China's major tungsten deposits and also has considerable deposits of molybdenum (useful in steel and high-temperature alloy production) and bismuth (used chiefly as a catalyst to increase fusibility of various metalic alloys). The folding of these mountains has exposed rich beds of non-ferrous metals as well as coal deposits. Pegmatite, an igneous rock with large, coarse crystals, interspersed in the granite contains a considerable number of rare elements including: beryllium and niobium (used in alloys to make tools), titanium (used in alloys for the aerospace industry and pigments), vanadium (for high-grade steel alloys), yttrium (used in alloys for optical glasses, special ceramics, and lasers), zirconium (used, as is niobium, as cladding in nuclear reactors) and scandium. Guangdong is currently the national leader or one of the leading provinces in the extraction of niobium, iron pyrites, bismuth, cadmium, germanium, glass sand, Iceland spar, kaolin, lead, monazite, phosphyttrite, porcelain clay, rock crystal, serpentine, shale oil, silver, tantalum, thallium tremolite, tin, tungsten, uranium, zinc, and zirconite. Other major minerals found include high-grade iron ore, limestone, and manganese. Some coal deposits are also mined as a local energy source.

THE GROWING ENERGY CRISIS

In 1991, Guangdong officially consumed just over 4.5 per cent of all energy used in Chinese industry but produced 8.7

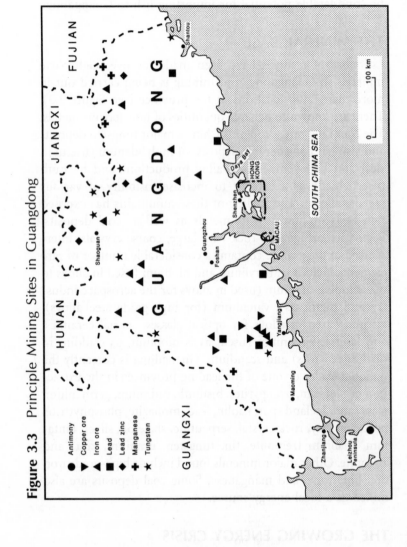

Figure 3.3 Principle Mining Sites in Guangdong

per cent of the gross industrial product (Figure 3.4). This energy consumption percentage is likely to be an understatement, as many Guangdong firms now have their own private generators. The amount of household energy consumed per capita has risen in recent years but was only about 60 per cent of the 1991 national average. This suggests that Guangdong suffers from energy shortages and that there is a good market for foreign energy investors.[17] In particular coal consumption per capita is low. Although there is some petroleum, shale oil, peat, natural gas, and renewable sources such as geothermal, solar, wind, and tidal energy potential in Guangdong, it is coal which dominates local energy generation with the proportion used for primary energy rising relative to oil and hydropower in recent years. There are worries ahead as it is predicted that by AD 2000 Guangdong's electricity demand will have risen to four times the 1990 level and most of this demand will have to be met by thermal power generation. In addition, power will have to be imported from western China which will require considerable investment in transmission lines.

Coal

Although coal is mined in the north and east, Guangdong is largely dependent upon imports from other provinces and in final energy consumption the percentage of coal relative to electricity is dropping. Between 1980 and 1991 electricity production in Guangdong went up 3.5 times but tonnes of local coal mined only rose by 16 per cent. The annual amount of electricity generated increased by 16.23 per cent between 1991 and 1992 alone.[18] In 1991, Guangdong mined nearly 9,331 thousand tonnes of coal ore (0.8 per cent of the national total) of which just over 40 per cent came from state-owned mines. Impurities in the state coal included 0.87 per cent rock and 19.57 per cent coal ash. As of 1992 over three-quarters of all new generating capacity under construction in the province was in nine thermal power plants.[19] Obviously coal production is not keeping up with needs, the quality of the coal is not that good, and future ability to meet local demand will

Figure 3.4 Guangdong's Energy Grid

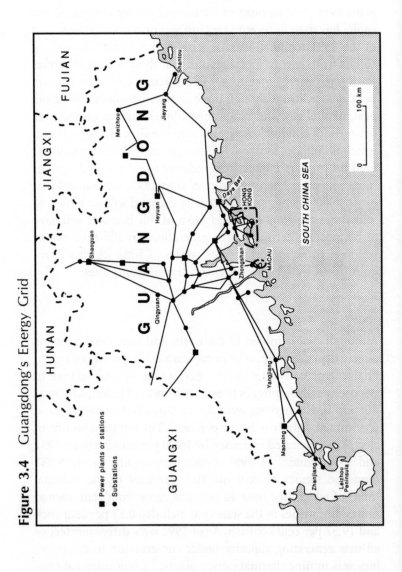

depend more upon inter-provincial transport improvements than upon increased local mining.

Oil

Oil has long been an energy source for which Guangdong has had to depend on outside sources. Onshore petroleum includes modest wells near Maoming in the west. Considerable potential is thought to exist on the continental shelf, including finds near the mouth of the Zhu River and at Beibuwan between Guangdong, Guangxi, Hainan, and Vietnam. As of 1992, close to 2.5 million tonnes of crude came from the offshore fields near the mouth of the Zhu River. It is thought that offshore production will peak around 1997.

As previously mentioned, Guangdong is one of the leading provinces in the extraction of shale oil, possessing the second largest deposits in China after Liaoning. Shale oil is concentrated in the Maoming area. The oil content of the shale is roughly 6 to 6.5 per cent with a heat value of 1,200 kilocalories/kilogram. Although as a source of energy it is inferior to crude oil or coal, there is thought to be large enough shale oil deposits in Guangdong to run a 3,000 megawatt electricity station for over one hundred years.[20]

Hydropower

With a fairly even geographic distribution of rivers, most regions in Guangdong have the potential to develop some hydroelectric power. In terms of per capita output, however, it is said that Guangdong and Hainan together have only 20 per cent of the national hydropower average. As of 1992 hydropower accounted for just over 25 per cent of the province's total energy production but only 8 per cent of primary energy consumption. Clearly it would be desirable to generate more hydroelectricity. As 1991 was a year of drought, the province only generated 1.8 million megawatt hours of electricity, nearly one-quarter less than the 1990 output. In 1992 there was an upswing in production but not to 1990 levels. The overall trend since the mid-1980s has been hydropower's decreasing role in Guangdong's energy mix. Although hydropower potential is not all that good, there is still some room for future development. Small-scale hydroelectric projects are still being undertaken, with an estimated 40 megawatts of power generation capacity added in 1991. Of new capacity under construction in 1992, only 22.2 per cent was in the form of hydropower stations.[21] Development of small-scale projects has been targeted to remote northern counties. In particular, the Bei River catchment in northern Guangdong has the greatest potential, followed by the Dong, Xi, and Han Rivers in that order. As in the rest of China, the hydropower resources are found in some of the least developed areas, whereas the heart of the Zhu River Delta, in particular the high energy-demand area of Guangzhou and Foshan, is short of potential.

Tidal Energy

Because the mouth of the Zhu River consists of a maze of water channels crisscrossing the delta, the tidal rise and fall is dispersed, limiting the ability to develop tidal energy when compared with other coastal estuaries further north. In general, as one moves inland along the river banks from the South China Sea, the difference in elevation between high and low tide drops rapidly, limiting the potential for tidal energy development to locations near the coast.

Nuclear Power

For decades, Hong Kong has worried about future energy shortages and Guangdong's ability to help the Colony overcome them. Hong Kong's desire for additional power and Guangdong's own strained capacity led to the decision to opt for nuclear power in the late 1970s. In 1985 Guangdong signed a contract with the Framatone Corporation, Electricité de France, and Hong Kong's China Light and Power to build two nuclear reactors with a 1,800 megawatt capacity at Daya Bay, 50 kilometres north-east of Hong Kong. One 900 megawatt reactor was in full commercial operation by February 1994, with the second one in operation from May 1995. In

October 1995 it was announced that Framatome, Electricité de France, and GEC-Alsthom will help build a nuclear plant at Ling'ao. About 70 per cent of the Daya Bay plant's electricity output is supposed to be supplied to Hong Kong with the remainder for Guangdong. In June 1991 the Guangdong government also approved the establishment of the Daya Bay Planning District and it has allocated space for heavy industry within the district in order to take advantage of the new local power source.

The building of a nuclear plant so close to Hong Kong has been a sensitive issue in the Territory, although the Hong Kong people cannot complain too much as they were supposed to be the major beneficiaries of the power generated.[22] The central government's plan to construct two additional reactors at Daya Bay has caused further worry. Hong Kong organizations as well as the Guangdong government have advocated building the two additional reactors at Yangjiang, 165 kilometres west of Macau. However, the Chinese had four International Atomic Energy Agency reviews of the Daya Bay site between 1990 and 1994; they have pointed out that according to the safety review conducted during the summer of 1993, the initial reactors at the Daya Bay plant will be well prepared to deal with emergencies.[23] Despite this, environmental worries continue to be expressed in Hong Kong and Macau. Problems which have kept China's first operating nuclear plant, the Chinese-built Qinshan plant in Zhejiang province, from operating at capacity suggest that Guangdong will need further foreign assistance to construct any new reactors.

The future energy picture for Guangdong in relation to Hong Kong and Macau is anything but clear. Daya Bay may have been perceived as necessary to supply energy for Hong Kong and the Yangjiang plant would be well situated to serve Macau, but growth of energy needs in Guangdong has exceeded that in the two enclaves. Hong Kong's China Power and Light is already selling increasing amounts of electricity to Guangdong. With energy-intensive industries moving out of Hong Kong and Macau into Guangdong and a new power plant being built in Hong Kong's New Territories, it is likely that less than the originally anticipated amount of Daya Bay's capacity will be transmitted to Hong Kong. Although massive reclamation projects will nearly double Macau's size by the early twenty-first century, the emphasis on non-energy-intensive industries will slow the growth of energy demand. There is also an increasing desire for energy efficiency in Hong Kong and Macau, especially in building construction. As a consequence, Daya Bay and any additional reactors will probably service Guangdong to a far greater degree than the future special economic regions of Hong Kong and Macau.

THE ENVIRONMENT

While both land degradation and pollution have been serious throughout China during the last several decades, most experts would argue that land degradation poses greater problems for China as a whole. In Guangdong, however, pollution has been the more serious of these two environmental threats due to the recent and rapid industrialization of the province. None the less, soil erosion is also a serious problem in the upland areas of Guangdong.

Soil Erosion

Soil erosion in the upland areas is not serious when compared with the situation in the Loess Plateau of northern China or the upper Chang (Yangtze) River Valley. Yet, one project study undertaken in Deqing county concluded that severe soil loss took place in areas adjacent to settlements and fields so that mass erosion from steep slopes often buried farm land on the valley floors. The cultivation of a medicinal plant, *Morinda officinalis*, which grows well on slopes exceeding 25°, was found to be the most erosion-prone land use in Deqing and testing of gullies revealed per-storm erosion rates which are amongst the highest in the world.[24] Aside from serious reduction of soil fertility, erosion has led to serious river siltation problems as well as to extension of the Zhu River Delta. For example, the Yuecheng River, a tributary of the Xi River, has had its bed raised by 3 metres since the 1950s and is now 1 metre higher than surrounding fields.

Efforts have been made to control erosion in Guangdong, especially since 1980. In 1991 alone, Guangdong authorities claim to have controlled soil erosion in a 780 square kilometre area. However, such efforts are not without criticism. Soil conservation programmes often were implemented on a trial and error basis with little attempt to understand the processes involved and there was no attempt to coordinate programmes in upland and lowland areas. Most of what was being done was due to the efforts of farmers, with local extension services only selecting and providing seeds for revegetation. Nobody was looking into the cost effectiveness of such soil conservation measures.[25]

Water Pollution

In Guangdong, as in much of China, water quality degradation is viewed as the most serious form of pollution because of the direct harm it causes to human life. In recent years organic pollution in the Meizhou section of the Han River and the Xi River, as well as various pollutants in the Jian River and Jiuzhou River in the west, have increased. Pollution is continuing to worsen in the sections of all rivers which pass through cities. While percentages of industrial waste water treated and industrial waste water reaching permissible emission standards have more than doubled between 1980 and 1992, the amount of waste water released also has doubled over the same period.

The government has reacted by passing regulations to protect waterways and drinking water. Many cities have recently set aside districts for protection of drinking water sources. In particular, effort has been made to preserve the quality of water going to Hong Kong and Shenzhen. There have been problems in managing water sources shared between two or more administrative units and efforts have been made to ensure more adequate protection. In industry close to two-thirds of waste water is now treated and half of the industrial waste water released reaches permissible standards. The situation for non-industrial waste water is no doubt worse.

Air Pollution

According to official statistics, the amount of particular pollutants dispersed into the air went up 2.7 times between 1985 and 1992. This figure could underestimate the total as it is doubtful that such statistics include all rural small-scale industries. Acid pollution costs have been heavy for Guangdong with rural losses due to reduced tree and crop yields and poisoned lands. Air pollution costs have been heavy for Guangdong with rural losses reported for the late 1980s as 2,300 million yuan per annum.[26] In terms of sulphur dioxide concentrations, the cities also tend to be maintaining the same sort of levels in recent years. The rate of industrial emissions into the atmosphere being treated has shown steady improvement, surpassing 80 per cent in 1992. Nitrogen oxide levels have been rising slightly due to the increased use of automobiles. Industrial dust emissions have been held around the 400,000 tonnes per annum mark since the mid-1980s while recovery of industrial dust has more than trebled. This demonstrates that while efforts to control pollution are significant, dust pollution levels are not going down. Rain pH values in 1991 averaged 3.67, a sign that acid pollution is fairly serious. The problem is particularly worrying because the warmer temperatures in Guangdong lead to more rapid conversion of SO_2 into sulphuric acid than occurs in central China, Western Europe, or eastern North America. Plant varieties which have been tested and found to resist various polluting airborne compounds are recommended for planting.[27]

Solid Wastes

The annual output of solid wastes grew about 1.7 times between 1980 and 1992. Reuse of solid wastes more than doubled over the same period. Again, however, economic growth has meant that more solid wastes are still piling up. As of

Table 3.4 Guangdong Citizen Complaints About the Environment

Year	1989	1990	1991
Letters of complaint received by environmental protection units	6,897	8,516	8,363
Visits to environmental protection units to lodge complaints	3,896	5,670	5,099

Source: *Guangdong Nianjian 1990*, p. 243; *1991*, p. 291; *1992*, p. 285.

1992, 20,270 square kilometres of land were occupied by solid wastes of which 2,550 square kilometres were arable land.

Noise Pollution

The expansion of transport and construction has led to high levels of noise pollution in Guangdong's cities. Efforts to control noise pollution with fines on a provincial-wide scale began in 1991. While some effort is being devoted to noise pollution it continues to have relatively low priority.

Environmental Management

Compared with other provinces, management of the environment appears to have been relatively good in Guangdong's urban areas. Guangzhou, which established its environmental protection organization in 1973, is proud that it has been able to maintain more or less steady levels of pollution as it experienced considerable economic growth during the 1980s.[28] As elsewhere in China, Guangdong has tried to initiate an environmental responsibility system in recent years: government officials must meet certain environmental targets or risk losing their jobs. Attempts to fine polluters have been stepped up. As Table 3.4 shows, there is a degree of active citizen consciousness, with about 40 per cent of letters voicing complaints about air pollution, 31 per cent about noise pollution and 13 per cent about water pollution in 1991.[29] If prosperity continues, however, there will be greater demand for a better urban environment and agricultural produce will come under closer scrutiny for levels of pollutants. The Hong Kong government has begun to demand the right to inspect vegetables grown in neighbouring Shenzhen despite claims by Shenzhen authorities that they are carrying out adequate surveillance. Land and soil conservation, however, will continue to be difficult due to the growing pressure of population upon the land.

TRANSPORTATION

Railways

As throughout China, the expansion of railways in Guangdong has not kept pace with demand. Only 420 kilometres of new lines were constructed between 1980 and 1992. The province faces coal supply shortages due to the inability of the railways to move enough coal from north China. During the period from 1986 to 1990, railways underwent a modest expansion, including improvements to the 540-kilometre long, double-tracked Hengyang–Guangzhou section of the Beijing–Guangzhou railway and construction of the 322-kilometre long Sanshui–Maoming line, later built with local government funds. In addition, the 147-kilometre line from Guangzhou to Shenzhen has been double-tracked and electrified. Since this last line became locally administered under a contract system, it has shown increased profits.

The Guangzhou–Shenzhen line is just one example of the major shift in railway management during the last decade. In 1980, 70 per cent of the total rail-network length was managed as national railways. In 1991 over half of the railway length in Guangdong became managed by local railways and the trend towards local management is continuing. Another major development in railway transport in the People's Republic began in March 1993 when the Pinghu–Nantouzhen railway went into operation. This 50-kilometre line in Shenzhen was the first joint Mainland–Hong Kong railway enterprise and signals the beginning of private capital investment in railways, once a very sensitive issue in China during the early twentieth century.

Current efforts will link other Guangdong ports into the Chinese rail grid. The Guangzhou–Zhuhai–Macau railway began construction in 1993 and a Guangzhou–Meizhou–Shantou railway is now under construction. During the period from 1991 to 1995, rails are to be improved on the electrified Guangzhou–Shenzhen line. The existing Beijing–Guangzhou mainline will be fully electrified, its rails will be improved, and a new marshalling station will be built for it in Guangzhou. Of major importance for Guangdong will be the new Beijing–Kowloon large-capacity railway which began construction in January 1993 and is to run parallel to the existing Beijing–Guangzhou line. This huge investment, with its annual freight capacity of 60 million tonnes, will help solve north–south transport bottlenecks. The line will be beneficial locally as the existing Beijing–Guangzhou line is under strain from overuse. It is said that 50 per cent of the goods which should move into Guangdong and 30 per cent of those which should be shipped north by rail cannot be moved now. The new railway will aid in getting goods from Guangzhou and the south of the province to the north. It is thought that construction of the Beijing–Kowloon line will allow the Guangdong economy to expand its growth rate by over 12 per cent throughout the 1990s.[30] However, the current network in Guangdong is so inadequate that it is highly unlikely the railways will be able to meet demand in the coming decade.

Roads

During the period from 1986 to 1992, 4,595 kilometres of road were constructed in Guangdong. Of the 58,000 kilometres of road in the province, over 98 per cent is paved and over 26 per cent is considered to be of excellent or good quality. This is roughly the same percentage of good quality roads as for Guangxi, but is significantly better than the proportion in neighbouring Fujian, Hainan, or Hunan. However, Guangdong's density of roads is about twice that of Guangxi, giving it by far the most dense and best road network in southern China. Like the railways, however, the road network is inadequate for Guangdong's needs, although the Guangzhou–Shenzhen super motorway, built by a Hong Kong investor, has improved transport along this major artery. Several road improvements are now under way including: the Guangzhou–Shantou highway, the Zhongshan–Panyu highway, the Huizhou–Shenzhen motorway, and the Chaozhou–Shantou–Chiwei–Zhangmutou motorway.

Finally, other planned roads include a new ring by-pass motorway around Guangzhou, another motorway extending from the provincial capital to Zhuhai and Macau, and a trunk road from Guangzhou to Zhanjiang and the southern tip of the Leizhou Peninsula, with a sea crossing to Hainan Island. These Chaozhou–Guangzhou–Zhanjiang and northern Guangdong–Guangzhou–Zhuhai links are part of a national trunk system now being constructed. The Guangzhou segments of these motorways are expected to become the most heavily used portions of the national network.[31]

Ports and Inland Waterways

As indicated in Table 3.5, the four major ports in Guangdong are Guangzhou, Zhanjiang, Shekou (Shenzhen), and Shantou, in that order. The differences between their capacities are considerable. All four are among China's original twenty-two coastal ports officially opened to foreign trade in 1983. In recent years, ports in Shenzhen and Shantou have expanded harbour capacity at a faster pace than their two larger competitors. One must remember that Hong Kong is still the major port in the region and its dominance has influenced attempts by Guangdong ports to expand.

One article has suggested that Zhanjiang is the only port in China which can ever become 'a second Hong Kong' based on the harbour's physical characteristics.[32] The water depth at Guangzhou harbour is only about nine metres and 20,000 tonne vessels must take advantage of tidal conditions to get in. Of the many harbours in Shenzhen, the one with the largest potential, Yantian, will have a capacity of 76 million tonnes as of the year 2020, but the water depth (15–20 metres) and

Table 3.5   Guangdong Transport Statistics, 1992

Mode	kilometres
Railway length	1,426
Road network length	55,883
Navigable inland waterways	10,857
Airline route length	169,491
Oil pipeline length	212
Passenger kilometres	*million passenger kilometres*
Railways	13,199
Road transport	19,102
Waterways	2,238
Airlines	8,105
Freight tonne kilometres	*million tonne kilometres*
Railways	23,934
Road transport	770
Waterways	265,948
Airlines	141
Pipelines	851
Port freight	*million tonnes*
Guangzhou	54.64
Zhanjiang	16.44
Shekou (Shenzhen)	6.56
Shantou	5.91
Chiwan	5.07
Mawan (Shenzhen)	1.48
Post offices	2,696
Telephone exchange capacity	3,050,000

Source: *Guangdong Tongji Nianjian 1993*, pp. 221, 227, 231.

area for establishing berths is not as good as at Zhanjiang. Another potential harbour for major port development is Daya Bay (Huizhou), which could eventually have a freight capacity of 100 million tonnes but so far has had little development to speak of.

In addition, there is competition for development of port facilities for the western side of the Zhu River Delta between the new Ka-Ho port on Macau's Coloane Island and the planned new port to its west at Gaolan in Zhuhai. The lack of a good port has made transport costs in and out of Macau more expensive than Hong Kong. To alleviate this problem, a contract to develop Ká-Hó Bay on the island of Coloane into a deep-water port with a capacity to handle 80,000 standard containers (TEU's) per annum was signed in 1988. Although the container terminal at Ká-Hó was officially inaugurated in December 1991, until 1993 local shippers were reluctant to move their operations from the Porto Interior on the Macau peninsula to the new port.[33] Future plans are to expand the total port area to 29 hectares and include construction of an industrial park. Although neighbouring Zhuhai's Gaolan port could have up to 100 berths to accommodate ships varying from 10,000 to 200,000 tones, it will take up to two decades to fully develop the facilities, as only two berths were under construction in 1993. In any case, the physical conditions at both Gaolan and Ká-Hó are quite inferior to Zhanjiang.

All Guangdong ports fall short of Zhanjiang in development potential. The size of the inner harbour at Zhanjiang is three times that of Rotterdam. The annual freight capacity of Zhanjiang can be expanded to 1,000 million tonnes. The inner harbour has a water depth of 13 to 23 metres and the depth of parts of the outer harbour can reach 40 metres. With islands serving as natural break-waters and no major river flowing in and depositing silt, the harbour is extremely well suited to further expansion. Much will hinge upon development of southwestern China, particularly Guangxi, Guizhou, and when the Nanning–Kunming railway is completed, Yunnan. In the case of Guangxi, however, the local authorities have been giving preferential treatment to shippers who use Guangxi ports.

Guangdong's inland waterway network has been largely stagnant in terms of expansion of length with only 49 kilometres added between 1980 and 1992. However, the amount of tonnage carried almost doubled over the same period and inland waterways have maintained their dominance in Guangdong's internal freight network (see Table 3.5). The inland waterway system has even been able to perform adequately under strain, as occurred during the 1991 drought. As development of Guangdong continues, however, one can expect to see greater growth in transport nodes which provide higher speed such as rail, road, and airlines.

Airlines

The development of airline service in Guangdong over the past decade has been phenomenal. There were seven times more kilometres of airline route length, almost nine times more passengers, and six times more freight carried in 1992 than in 1980. No other mode of transport comes close to that sort of expansion during the past twelve years. Moreover, growth continues to be higher than for other modes. There are problems of airport congestion, both in terms of the ability of certain airports to handle capacity and in the case of the Zhu River Delta, perhaps too great a geographical concentration with airports in Guangzhou, Zhuhai, Shenzhen, Hong Kong, and Macau by the turn of the century.

Asian airlines have generally not had trouble attracting passengers during the recent recession and China's domestic services are virtually unaffected. Therefore, the future for airline expansion in Guangdong should be excellent and no doubt the facilities will continue to expand in the coming decades. After the breakup of the monolithic national carrier CAAC in 1985, Guangzhou-based China Southern emerged as the country's second largest airline with fifty-eight planes as of 1993. There are also a number of smaller domestic airlines, such as Hainan Airlines, which serve destinations in Guangdong. Accidents such as China Southern's 24 November 1992 Boeing 737–300 crash near Guilin, however, do not inspire confidence. There is also a shortage of good quality domestic staff which suggests that China Southern may have to hire foreign crews. So far, however, the Chinese have avoided this and have also kept foreign companies flying into China to a minimum so that foreign airlines' opportunities in Guangdong (excluding Hong Kong-based companies such as Dragon Air and Air Macau) are likely to be limited to joint training programmes for the immediate future.

MARKETS AND URBANIZATION

Since the beginning of the open reforms in the late 1970s a considerable amount of specialized marketing has re-emerged in Guangdong, especially in the Zhu River Delta. Examples include the Nanhai Xiqiao cloth market, the Dongguan banana wholesale market, the Panyu Shiqiao household electric goods market, the Shunde Chencun fresh flower market, as well as the Shenzhen stock market.[34] In addition there are local markets for all sorts of consumption products, industrial products, construction materials, and property. It is fair to say that marketing in Guangdong is amongst the most sophisticated in China. This re-emergence of markets was accompanied by a rapid rate of urbanization.

Discussions of urbanization in China are hampered by problems in defining what is and what is not a city and its urban population. For a start, all of Guangdong at the prefectural level is divided into twenty municipalities (*diji shi*), eighteen of which are municipalities with urban wards (*shequ de shi*).[35] These municipalities with urban wards also have counties (*xian*) under their administration. Guangdong also has two municipalities without wards (*bushequ de shi*) at the prefectural level: Dongguan and Zhongshan. In any case, Guangdong's prefectural-level municipalities do not correspond to urban areas. They simply are indicators at the national level of prefectures which are significantly urban. In addition to these prefectural-level municipalities, there are six county-level municipalities which come under the administration of one of the prefectural-level municipalities.[36] Below this there are 1,321 towns (*zhen*) in the Guangdong urban-administrative hierarchy.

By official definition, all of the ward population of the municipalities with urban wards is considered urban, but only the population of street committee areas (*jiedao weiyuanhui*) of the municipalities without wards is considered urban. Table 3.6 shows the total non-agricultural population for municipalities without wards and therefore, probably overstates their urban population. In contrast, the urban population of the larger municipalities with wards, such as Guangzhou, Shenzhen, and Zhuhai is underestimated due to the non-inclusion of 'temporary population'. For example, according to the *Shenzhen Tongji Nianjian 1993*, over 69 per cent of Shenzhen's 1992 total population was 'temporary'. In the city of Guangzhou, there may be up to 0.5 million imported labourers. This population is not included in Table 3.6. Therefore, the data in Table 3.6 excludes much of the urban population in the larger cities and does not include the urban population found in smaller centres.

We know that urbanization in Guangdong has been rapid in recent years and that this has led to a reduction in arable land and localized water shortages. Of the sixteen largest cities listed in Table 3.6, twelve are located in the Zhu River catchment and two are coastal ports, leaving Shaoguan and Zhaoqing as the only large cities in the interior. However, both Shaoguan and Zhaoqing are located on tributaries of the Zhu River and therefore, are also in highly accessible positions. While Guangzhou remains the key city within the province, it faces severe competition for economic supremacy in the future from an integrated Hong Kong–Shenzhen urban area. Guangzhou will acquire additional prestige when its planned metro underground railway system is completed. None the less, both of these conglomerations, plus the Macau–Zhuhai urban area, can expect significant population growth in the coming decades.

The urbanization process is accompanied by the growth of social problems, especially in the large coastal cities. Guangzhou, which experienced a higher inflation rate than the national average during the first quarter of 1993, is particularly susceptible to social disruption. The rich cities of the Zhu

Table 3.6 Non-agricultural Population of Guangdong
Municipalities and the Populations of Hong Kong and
Macau, 1992 (in thousands of persons)

Hong Kong (1991 total pop.)	5,755.0
Guangzhou	2,995.6
Shantou	615.4
Shenzhen	472.8
Zhanjiang	432.9
Macau	380.9
Shaoguan	374.0
Foshan	327.7
Dongguan	327.1
Zhongshan	309.9
Shunde (administered by Foshan)	282.4
Jiangmen	255.3
Nanhai (administered by Foshan)	250.2
Xinhui (administered by Jiangmen)	240.0
Zhaoqing	221.5
Zhuhai	212.7
Maoming	211.8
Panyu (administered by Guangzhou)	210.3
Chaozhou	205.0
Huizhou	198.8
Yangjiang	188.0
Taishan (administered by Jiangmen)	174.9
Jieyang	152.6
Meizhou	142.8
Qingyuan	141.9
Heyuan	138.8
Shanwei	121.6
Yunfu (administered by Zhaoqing)	84.6
Total non-agricultural population in municipalities	*9,288.6*
Total non-agricultural population in Guangdong	*16,408.0*
Total urban population (chengshi renkou) *in 1990 census*	*15,638.7*

Source: *Guangdong Tongji Nianjian 1993*, pp. 135, 467–70.

River Delta have the greatest job mobility, which has given their residents more freedom in their lifestyles than people in most others areas of China. There have been strikes in Zhuhai and labour unrest elsewhere. Crime rates have soared.[37] So far these problems have not led to a backlash, but they do give Guangdong the image of being the most 'spiritually polluted' province in China.

Of Guangdong's other cities, Zhaoqing, located at the junction of the Xi River and the new Sanshui–Maoming railway, is particularly well placed for further growth. This city should emerge as a major freight transfer node between Zhanjiang and southern Guangxi to the west and routes to northern China, Guangzhou, Hong Kong, and Macau to the east, with the upper Xi River valley as a new development hinterland to its northwest. We have already noted Zhanjiang's development potential in terms of its port facilities. Other cities which are likely to continue experiencing rapid urbanization include Shantou and the smaller cities located in the Zhu River Delta, including Foshan, Dongguan, Zhongshan, Shunde, Nanhai, Panyu, and Taishan.

SPECIAL ECONOMIC ZONES AND OTHER FREE-TRADE ZONES

Coastal Open Belt

As of 1991, seventeen municipalities (*shi*) and forty-four counties (*xian*) coterminous to the coast and comprising 49.1 per cent of Guangdong's area and 71 per cent of its population, were open to foreign trade. The rest of the province looks with envy at this belt and aspires to join its ranks. Within the open belt, there are specific zones which enjoy preferential treatment in foreign trade: Special Economic Zones (*jingji tequ*), open cities (*kaifang chengshi*), economic and technical development zones (*jingji jishu kaifaqu*), and free-trade zones (*baoshuiqu*).

The Special Economic Zones: Pioneers of Foreign Trade

Guangdong is home to three of China's five Special Economic Zones (SEZs): Shenzhen (1993 estimated population 1,220,200, area 327.5 sq. km.), Zhuhai (1992 pop. 292,000, area 121 sq. km.), and Shantou (1992 pop. 894,000, area 234 sq. km.). All three were founded in 1980, primarily to attract capital from Hong Kong, Macau, and overseas. A comparison with Table 3.2 reveals that the Special Economic Zones make up only a small portion of the Territory of their respective municipalities. All three SEZs have experienced considerable growth, but Shantou in particular has seen very rapid expansion in the early 1990s after lagging behind Shenzhen in the 1980s. In terms of 1992 foreign exports measured in US dollars, Shenzhen exported three times more than Shantou which only exported 1.6 times more than Zhuhai. For foreign imports, Shenzhen SEZ brought in over twice the value of Shantou which imported slightly over twice the amount of Zhuhai. After having been criticized since their creation in the early 1980s for not having attracted enough high-technology direct foreign investment, but rather functioning as low-tech, labour-intensive processing zones for Hong Kong and Macau, these three zones are now attracting high-technology direct foreign investment.

In terms of total foreign capital, Shenzhen SEZ used about twice the amount of Zhuhai during 1992 which used under one-half times again as much as Shantou. Shenzhen stands out in that the SEZ accounts for only around one-third of actual investment in Shenzhen Municipality whereas the other two SEZs account for the vast majority of funds used in the municipalities of Zhuhai and Shantou. Infrastructural investment in all three municipalities has been considerable, but the Shenzhen Special Economic Zone and Shenzhen Municipality remain at a higher level of economic activity than Zhuhai or Shantou.

During the last couple of years, however, Zhuhai and Shantou have been undertaking infrastructural investments in order to boost their ability to attract foreign investment. Shenzhen has developed a stock market in its bid to become China's financial centre. Ultimately, local natural resources, aside from location and harbour development potential, have little role to play in the development of Guangdong's special economic zones. The future is bright for these SEZs, no longer because of preferential treatment since many of the privileges exclusively given to them in the 1980s are now common to many cities in China, but because of their early acquisition of modern trading techniques and their locations and connections with Hong Kong, Macau, and overseas Chinese communities.

Open Cities: Early Leaders in China's Development Drive

In addition to the Special Economic Zones, Guangdong also has two of China's fourteen so-called open cities which were opened in 1984: Guangzhou and Zhanjiang. Although both these cities have been discussed elsewhere, it is worth noting that Guangzhou is the economically, as well as politically and demographically, more important with over eight times Zhanjiang's gross value of industrial output in 1992. The selection of these cities as open cities was based upon their historical foundation of overseas contact and therefore, their ability to stimulate foreign trade and to bring in foreign investment through preferential treatment. It is also hoped that they will continue to attract tourists and establish successful economic and technical development zones.

Economic and Technical Development Zones

Each of these open cities possess an economic and technical development zone (ETDZ). The purpose of these zones is to help the open cities upgrade industries, balance their industrial structure, and develop an export orientation. In practice, these ETDZs seem to be little more than mini-special economic zones, although the range of goods which can be produced is more limited. By the end of 1991, the Guangzhou

Economic and Technical Development Zone (9.6 sq. km.) had 209 enterprises either in production or committed to investment and employed 17,984 people, whereas the Zhanjiang ETDZ (9.2 sq. km.) had 106 enterprises and employed 6,086 workers. The Guangzhou ETDZ is located at the confluence of the Zhu River and the northern main channel of the Dong River, about 35 kilometres from the centre of Guangzhou. There are plans to expand the zone to include more industrial belts and a residential area for workers. The Zhanjiang ETDZ is located between the Xiashan and Chikan wards of the city. Industrial development here includes food processing and machinery works. As of 1992, 68.7 per cent of the area in the Guangzhou ETDZ was already developed, whereas only 28.3 per cent of the Zhanjiang ETDZ was developed. The industrial output of the Guangzhou Economic and Technical Development Zone is roughly twice that of Zhanjiang in renminbi terms, although exports from the Guangzhou ETDZ in US dollar terms are almost four times that of Zhanjiang. As previously noted, Zhanjiang has considerable development potential as a harbour. However, so far the economic and technical development zone level of preferential treatment has not been enough to kick-start Zhanjiang's economy to the point where the port can develop to compete with Guangzhou or Hong Kong.

Free-trade Zones

In 1991 and 1992 three free-trade zones were established in Guangdong. This is a significant number when we realize that there were only thirteen such free-trade zones in all China as of mid-1993. The smallest free-trade zone in China is the Shatoujiao zone in Shenzhen (0.2 sq. km.) which was established in September 1992. By mid-1993, sixty-two enterprises were in operation with the focus of the zone being on high-tech processing projects. External investment, particularly from Hong Kong, Macau, and Taiwan, dominates. There is another zone in Shenzhen known as the Futian free-trade zone. A 1.4 square kilometre zone in Guangzhou began operation in May 1993. The emphasis in the Guangzhou free-trade zone is on entrepôt trading. The zone is right next to the Guangzhou Economic and Technical Development Zone with the hope that the two can integrate.

It is too early to tell how successful the free-trade zones will be. As they offer duty-free facilities and should speed import-export procedures, however, there is every reason to suspect that they will develop faster than the economic and technical development zones. Nationally, there have been problems standardizing the administration and controlling the number of places selected to become free-trade zones. The central government seems intent on limiting their number to thirteen for the time being.

The plethora of economic zones within Guangdong shows the complexity and changing character of China's economic geography. What can be safely said at this stage is that these various zones tend to be concentrated along the coast in the most developed parts of Guangdong. Although the various zones are gradually merging and have begun to lose their unique privileges shortly after they are created, the newer free-trade zones could further heighten differences between the coast and the interior. It is the proximity and interaction of these preferential zones with Hong Kong and Macau that has created the greatest economic dynamo in contemporary China.

INTEGRATION WITH HONG KONG AND MACAU

The trend since 1978 has been for ever increasing integration of Guangdong with Hong Kong and Macau. Guangdong is the major supplier of water, electricity, and agricultural produce to Hong Kong and Macau and also supplies semi-finished goods for further processing and for export. In dry years such as 1991, the need to supply Hong Kong and Macau with energy and fresh food has put a considerable strain on the resources available for the province. Hong Kong investment in Guangdong is big. 90 per cent of the members of the Federation of Hong Kong Industries now have factories in the province and

Hong Kong accounts for 80 per cent of the foreign investment in Guangdong. There are an estimated 725,000 people in Guangdong working for Hong Kong companies (among over 3 million people in the region who are directly engaged in outward processing for Hong Kong). This growing interconnection has transformed the Zhu River Delta into the core of the so-called 'Greater China' economic sphere.

THE ZHU RIVER DELTA OPEN COASTAL ECONOMIC ZONE AND THE DELTA

The Zhu River Delta's areal extent is different depending on whether one uses physical or economic conditions as the basis for delimitation. For development purposes the delta is defined in economic-administrative terms as the Zhu River Delta Open Coastal Economic Zone (*Zhujiang Sanjiaozhou Jingji Kaifangqu*). The Zhu River Delta Open Coastal Economic Zone was one of the first nationally established when it was promulgated in February 1985. It was expanded in 1987 and now is composed of seven municipalities and twenty-one counties for a total area of over 45,000 square kilometres and close to 17 million people or slightly more than one-quarter of Guangdong's area and population.[38] As already noted, it is the hub of Guangdong with excellent land for agriculture (over 900,000 hectares of arable land) and good communications. In particular, Foshan, Zhongshan, and Jiangmen have developed externally-oriented ports in their own right with good connections to Hong Kong and Macau. In 1992 the zone had a total actual foreign investment of US$1,891 million, over 38 per cent of Guangdong's total.

The development strategy for the 1990s is to stress development of the service sector within the delta. Emphasis is to be placed upon research, education, financial markets, information technology, and real-estate development. From this core it is hoped that development will first 'trickle out' to the eastern and western coastal 'wings' of the province (principally Shantou-Chaozhou to the east and Zhanjiang-Maoming to the west) and then spread to the north—particularly to growth pole areas such as Shaoguan and along the Xi River upstream from Zhaoqing.

Within the delta there are in fact four distinct development regions. First of all, there is Hong Kong and Macau. Within Guangdong proper there is Shenzhen and Zhuhai, Guangzhou and the riverine open cities, and finally the rest of the Zhu River Delta Open Coastal Economic Zone. In the riverine open cities, there has been a tendency for duplication of development rather than coordinated economic specialization. Infrastructural development interlinking these cities such as the Guangzhou–Zhuhai–Macau railway also regrettably have been delayed. Yet, as we have noted in the discussion of markets, some specialization has occurred and the Zhu River Delta as a whole should remain China's key economic region for at least a decade despite major investment to develop the Chang (Yangtze) River Delta.

THE FUTURE FOR GUANGDONG

Guangdong has been at the forefront of China's development strategy, having a majority of the Special Economic Zones, two important open cities, one of the first and most important coastal economic zones, and a complement of economic and technical development zones and free-trade zones. During the past decade and a half, Guangdong's open coastal area has expanded considerably and virtually all of China must look to the province's economic record with envy. Within Guangdong, however, not all areas have profited from the open policy to the same degree. To confront the problem of growing regional discrepancies, the provincial government began to organize meetings in the mid-1980s to discuss the economic problems of the interior or 'mountainous district' (*shanqu*). The forty-nine administrative units designated as part of this mountainous district make up 63 per cent of the population and about 41 per cent of Guangdong's total area and cultivated area. The mountainous district, however, only produced 15.8 per cent of the province's 1991 gross output value of industry and agriculture. In terms of gross value of agricultural output, the figure was a more respectable 37.6 per cent, yet the gross industrial output amounted to only 10.3 per cent of the provincial total. The average income for a peasant in the mountainous district was just slightly above 40 per cent of the provincial average, which gives us at least some idea of the current level of discrepancy.

Yet the picture for mountainous Guangdong is not all that bleak. Prosperity is beginning to trickle into the interior and the situation in the mountainous district of Guangdong is not serious when compared to problems in other provinces. If the Guangdong government is allowed to retain more of the funds that its coastal area generates in the future, no doubt some of these funds will be used to further develop the mountainous interior. Lower wages in the interior should encourage more industrial activities to move inland and there is a natural resource base which can be used for some heavy industry. Given that industrial growth in Guangdong has not been led by mining or heavy industries, however, transport links, along with wage levels and labour skills, are more likely to determine which areas develop in the future.

NOTES

1. The coldest area is found in Lianshan Zhuang-Yao Autonomous County which has an average annual temperature of only 18 °C.
2. The mean level of precipitation per annum is 1,887.9 millimetres. The annual extremes vary between 1,000 to 2,600 millimetres.
3. The general elevation of the Nan Ling is about 1,000 metres but peaks go as high as 1,900 metres above sea level. Cold air flows enter Guangdong on average ten times a year. Usually these air flows are above 0 °C. Yet under appropriate conditions, they can induce frost. When cold air does penetrate it usually follows the river valleys or comes southward through the Taiwan Straits.
4. In the republican era and on Nationalist Chinese maps published in Taiwan today, the coastal counties of Guangxi are shown as part of Guangdong.
5. According to Wu Yuwen, et al. eds., *Guangdong Sheng Jingji Dili* (Economic geography of Guangdong province), Beijing: Xinhua Chubanshe, 1985, p. 15. 42.4 per cent of the province's agricultural land is located in the mountainous and hilly areas.

6. The quarternary period is the most recent geologic era, beginning roughly two million years ago.

7. Wu, *Guangdong Sheng Jingji Dili*, p. 17.

8. The pH levels in Guangdong's soils are normally between 4.5 and 6.5.

9. Wu, *Guangdong Sheng Jingji Dili*, p. 32.

10. Ibid., p. 35.

11. Increasingly new species of trees have been introduced from overseas as a result of international contacts. Stanley Dennis Richardson, *Forests and Forestry in China: Changing Patterns of Resource Development*, Washington and Covelo, Calif.: Island Press, 1990, pp. 211–13 notes that although *Eucalyptus* spp. were first introduced into Guangdong in the late nineteenth century, new selections have come from Australia since the 1970s. This fast-growing species is being used as construction material, fuelwood, and sawed timber. However, there is some environmental controversy around the widespread use of *Eucalyptus* spp., as it uses up a significant amount of water and nutrients. As Guangdong is not yet facing a water crisis and there is need for the timber growth that *Eucalyptus* spp. generates, the tree has a continued role to play. However, over-planting could affect soil and water conservation in certain areas.

12. Derek Elsom and Martin Haigh, 'Progress and Pollution', *The Geographical Magazine*, 58, 12 (1986): 643, visited the latosols region of Dianbai County and were told that deforestation in that area during twentieth century increased soil erosion by a factor greater than 3,400.

13. Elsom and Haigh, 'Progress and Pollution', p. 644, were told that a person caught chopping down trees in Sanshui County was responsible for planting three new ones and if these died the person was to be imprisoned. How often authorities in rural areas have been able and willing to enforce such rules is difficult to say.

14. *Zhongguo Linye Nianjian* Bianji Weiyuanhui, ed., *Zhongguo Linye Nianjian 1988* (China forestry yearbook), Beijing: Zhongguo Linye Chubanshe, 1988, p. 70.

15. Clive S. K. Lau, 'Pine Wilt Disease and the Ecology and Life Cycle of the Pinewood Nematode *Bursaphelenchus Xylophilus*', *Asia-Pacific Uplands*, 2 (1991): 15.

16. Bao Yuhuang, 'Qianlun Zhu Jiang Sanjiaozhou Diqu Jingji Fazhan yu Hezuo' (A brief discourse on the Zhu River Delta region's economic development and co-operation), *Gang Ao Jingji*, 126 (1993): 26.

17. China only fully opened the energy sector to foreign investment in 1992. One Hong Kong firm, however, Gordon Wu's Hopewell Holdings, had built the first and only foreign built-operated-transferred power project in China, Shajiao B (2 × 350 megawatts) in Shenzhen as early as 1987. Other thermal power plants built with foreign investment are: Zhujiang (2 × 300 megawatts) and Shajiao C (3 × 660 megawatts).

18. China, Ministry of Electric Power and Ministry of Water Resources.

113

Electric Power Industry in China, Beijing: Epoch Printing Co., Ltd., 1993, p. 57. As of 1992, total installed generating capacity amounted to 10,825 megawatts.

19. Ibid.

20. Wu, *Guangdong Sheng Jingji Dili,* p. 237.

21. China, Ministry of Electric Power and Ministry of Water Resources, *Electric Power Industry in China,* p. 57.

22. As of 1991, Guangdong and Hong Kong's capacity to exchange electricity reached 750 megawatts after work was completed on Shenzhen to Yuen Long and Shenzhen to Fan Ling transmission networks. A critique of the Daya Bay Nuclear Station and its impact on Hong Kong can be found in Xianggang Dazhuan Jiaoshi Guanzhu Daya Wan Hedianchang Xiaozu, ed., *Hezi Fadian Daya Wan Jihua Mianmianguan* (Nuclear electricity: a view of the Daya Bay plan), Hong Kong: Ming Bao Chubanshe, 1987.

23. 'Daya Bay Project Nearly Completed', *Beijing Review,* 36, 27 (5–11 July 1993): 5–6 and 'Daya Wan Hedian: Qingjie Nengyuan, Youzhu Huanbao' (Daya Bay nuclear power: clean energy, an aid to environmental protection), *Cheng Bao* (5 February 1994): 37.

24. Luk Shiu-hung and Yao Qingyin, 'Soil Erosion and Land Management in the Granitic Regions of Guangdong Province, South China', final report submitted to the International Development Research Centre of Canada, University of Toronto and Guangzhou Institute of Geography 1990, pp. 10–11, 34, 43–4.

25. Ibid., p. 2.

26. Eduard B. Vermeer, 'Management of Environmental Pollution in China: Problems and Abatement Policies', *China Information,* 5, 1 (1990): 43. The Guangdong losses were assessed as 61 per cent in forestry, 26 per cent in crop losses, and 13 per cent in damaged farm land.

27. For example, Elsom and Haigh, ('Progress and Pollution', pp. 640–1) note the planting of 17,000 trees around a Guangzhou chemical works to combat air pollution in the mid-1980s. These trees supposedly reduced chlorine concentrations in the area by 20 per cent in two years.

28. According to quotes in Huang Guangui, 'Guangzhou Shi Huanbaorenyuan de Huanbao Yishi'. (The environmental consciousness of Guangzhou Municipality's environmental protection staff) in Liu Rong, ed. *Zhonghua Jingji Xiezuo Xitonglun* (Study of the Greater China economic co-operation system), Hong Kong: Sanlian Shudian, 1993, p. 294. A Guangzhou source states that the Guangzhou gross national product increased 157 per cent between 1985 and 1990 and the gross industrial product went up 84 per cent, while the quality of the environment supposedly underwent no degradation.

29. *Guangdong Nianjian 1990,* p. 243; *1991,* p. 291; *1992,* p. 285.

30. Wu Naitao, 'China's 10 Key Railway Projects', *Beijing Review,* 36, 42 (18–24 October 1993): 19.

31. 'China's Expanding Highway Networks', *Beijing Review*, 36, 40 (4–10 October 1993): 13. This is in reference to four national trunk lines. The two east-west trunk motorways go across central China.

32. Yang Xin, 'Dier ge "Xianggang" Zai Nali?' (Where is the second "Hong Kong"?), *Gang Ao Jingji*, 129 (June 1993): 5–6.

33. According to Paulo Coutinho, 'Um Porto-mar no Delta,' *Macau*, 2, 13 (Maio 1993), p. 7, this problem began to be resolved in spring 1992 by the merger of some of the Porto Interior companies into the Ká-Hó operations. In 1992 Macau handled 72,000 TEUs. Approximately 20,000 TEUs were handled by Ká-Hó port.

34. Bao Yuhuang, 'Qianlun Zhu Jiang Sanjiaozhou Diqu Jingji Fazhan yu Hezuo', p. 26.

35. Although it cannot be taken as a measure of urbanization because some counties contain urban areas and often a considerable area within a municipality is by most definitions rural, in 1985 Guangdong was divided into only nine municipalities and three 'rural' districts (*diqu*) at the prefectural level. Richard Kirkby, 'Dilemmas of Urbanization: Review and Prospects', in Denis Dwyer, ed., *China: The Next Decades*, Harlow, England: Longman Scientific & Technical, 1994, p. 131 notes that since 1986 towns (*zhen*) in China have been allowed to become designated as municipalities as long as they have a non-agricultural population of 60,000 and an annual gross product of over 200 million yuan.

36. In 1985 there were five such municipalities.

37. Carl Goldstein, 'Guangdong's Economy Booms, but the Crime Rate Soars', *Far Eastern Economic Review*, 156, 14 (8 April 1993): 15–16.

38. Figures for the Zhu River Delta Open Coastal Economic Zone vary from source to source. Those given here are from the *Guangdong Nianjian 1992*, pp. 386–7. For example, *Zhongguo Tizhi Gaige yu Duiwai Kaifang Dacidian* (A Comprehensive dictionary of Chinese system reform and opening to the outside world), Chengdu: Sichuan Kexue Chubanshe, 1992, p. 1005, states that there are eight municipalities and twenty-four counties in the 46,100-square-kilometre Zhu River Delta Open Coastal Economic Zone.

4 HUMAN RESOURCES AND THE IMPACT OF REFORMS

Brian Hook and Lee Wing On

The quest to modernize China has been under way since the closing decades of the nineteenth century. It took almost a century of political and economic vicissitudes for the quest to yield substantive and apparently irreversible results. Provided no unforeseen and enduring calamity befalls China under a post—Deng Xiaoping leadership, a three-dimensional framework, comprising developments in the economy and consequentially, in the polity and human resources, seems certain to characterize the historiography of the closing decades of the twentieth century.

Beginning in the late 1970s, spurred on by economic and political necessity, the first arising from implications of population growth, the second from the loss of political credibility following the debacle of the Cultural Revolution, the Communist Party of China (CPC) introduced reforms in major economic sectors and re-launched China into world trade. Although the reform policies were not accompanied by substantial structural reform in the political arena, they were to have dramatic results in both the economic and political context. Nowhere in China have the results been so conspicuous as in the southeastern province of Guangdong.

The remarkable effects of the Reform and Open Door policy in Guangdong, as compared to other beneficiaries such as Fujian province, Shanghai and the Yangtze Valley, and Beijing–

Tianjin, was achieved by both political design and historical coincidence. The former was epitomized by the decision to create Special Economic Zones (SEZs) and to locate three of them in Guangdong and one in Fujian. The aim was to induce, through incentives, foreign direct investment in technology, to promote modern production through various forms of joint venture, and to gain revenue from exports. Besides export revenues, there would be considerable spin-off in terms of foreign direct investment (FDI), technology transfer, and enhanced employment. The historical coincidence, on the other hand, lay in the existence of a highly developed neighbour, Hong Kong.

The existence of British Hong Kong was a unique feature since it would soon revert to China. Not only did its political and constitutional status face imminent transition, but its economy had also reached a major turning point. In the late 1970s, the question for Hong Kong was how to proceed from the successful manufacturing base created in the 1960s and 1970s, when China's isolation and planned economy had precluded the continuation of Hong Kong's historical entrepôt trade.

The economic effect of the Reform and Open Door policies on Guangdong, in particular of the creation of the SEZs, is evident elsewhere in this study. Suffice to say that its general regional impact was the rapid and sustained development of a unique symbiotic relationship with Hong Kong. This relationship put the human and natural resources of Guangdong at the disposal of capital, manufacturing, management, and marketing expertise channelled from or through Hong Kong. In less than two decades, while remaining separate political entities under different sovereigns, the economies of the two became significantly integrated, with Hong Kong interests employing a very large number of people in Guangdong.

As the following sections demonstrate, this integrative process has had and continues to have a profound effect on human resource supply and demand in Guangdong. The Dengist political initiatives that led to the liberalization of the Chinese economy, and the opportunistic restructuring of the Hong

Kong economy had far-reaching consequences. First, the bulk of Hong Kong's manufacturing base was relocated in Guangdong, creating a huge demand on local human resources. Second, the service economy developed in Hong Kong itself, solving the problem as to whether the manufacturing base should follow the lead of Japan and Taiwan by going towards high-tech, high value-added production. Third, Hong Kong was poised to service not only the adjoining economy but the whole of Southern China, with a concomitant demonstration effect, as it resumed the role of a turn-of-the-century, state-of-the-art entrepôt.

Against this background, Guangdong gathered momentum for reform in 1978, when the central government of China adopted the Reform and Open Door policy. Having benefited from the special policy which allowed the province to embark on economic experiments, Guangdong has been and remains at the forefront of reform over the past decade and a half. This chapter studies the impact of the liberalization of the Guangdong economy on human resources. It first investigates how the change in the enterprise system affected employment practices and the emergence of labour mobility and migration. Having established the main quantitative aspects in the pattern of supply and demand related to the liberalization of the economy, the chapter examines how the qualitative and quantitative needs for human resources, relevant to the changing economy, are met. The chapter concludes by discussing the impact of the changing economy on Guangdong's education system, illustrating how developments in the education system have reflected the liberalization of the economy.

THE LIBERALIZATION OF THE LABOUR MARKET

The liberalization of the economy has led to the development of an open and free labour market in Guangdong. The 1980s witnessed the weakening of state-owned enterprises on the one hand, and the growth of non-state-owned enterprises on the other. The non-state sector includes collective enterprises

Table 4.1 The Composition of Industrial Production Value by Type of Ownership in Guangdong (in per cent)[1]

| Type of Ownership | Guangdong | | | | China |
	1980	1985	1988	1989	1989
State-owned	63.0	52.5	41.2	37.5	56.1
Collective	26.6	30.5	31.0	28.6	35.7
Private, Village	8.5	12.4	15.7	16.6	4.8
Joint forms*	1.9	4.6	12.2	17.3	3.6
Total	100	100	100	100	100

* Joint forms include joint ventures of state-owned enterprise and collective enterprise, or collective enterprise and private enterprise.

(that is, owned by local governments and units), private enterprises, foreign enterprises, and various types of joint ventures. As shown in Table 4.1, while state enterprises accounted for almost two-thirds of the total provincial industrial production value in 1980, their share was reduced to just over one-third by 1989. In contrast, the production value of the non-state sector grew from just over one-third to almost two-thirds of the total provincial figure. The growth in the output value of private enterprises and joint ventures is even more notable, with some two-fold and eight-fold increases respectively over the decade.

The growth of the non-state sector has had significant implications for the employment structure. Until the introduction of the new labour law at the beginning of 1995, and initiatives to improve welfare for employees, government intervention in the employment practices of the non-state enterprises was minimal. Such intervention was confined to the imposition of levies such as labour management fees, wage adjustment tax, and social infrastructure charges. Subsequently, a comprehensive contract system of employment has developed even in state-owned enterprises. Wage is therefore linked directly to profit, and the welfare of staff and workers is then tied to enterprise performance.[2]

Enterprise managers began experimenting with the contract system in Shenzhen in 1983, and the State Council formally introduced the system in 1986. By the end of the year, about 7 per cent (520,000 workers) of the province's state and collective workforce, became part of the system. Workers commonly received contracts for terms ranging from one to five years, and in practice, they could leave or be terminated in the middle of the contract. The introduction of the contract system severely affected the pre-existing life-tenure system. Employment in Guangdong is increasingly characterized by free choice on both the supply and demand sides.[3] It is estimated that the proportion of labour employed through market mechanisms was as high as 85 per cent by 1991 in cities and towns.[4] By the early 1990s, over 50 per cent of enterprises in Guangdong were managed according to the market situation rather than by administrative directives.[5]

LABOUR MOBILITY AND CHANGES IN THE STRUCTURE OF EMPLOYMENT

Labour mobility has been closely associated with the introduction of market mechanisms and the change in employment structure in Guangdong. As shown in Table 4.2, the proportion of the labour force in the primary industry sector dropped by 20 per cent between 1978 and 1989, whereas the labour force in the secondary and tertiary industry sectors grew by 10 per cent respectively.

During the eleven years between 1978 and 1989, an annual average of 2.9 per cent or an overall total of 6.08 million employees in Guangdong moved from agriculture to other sectors. Of these, 55 per cent or 3.31 million moved to the industrial sector, and the remaining 45 per cent or 2.77 million to the service sector. If the Reform and Open Door period is divided into two stages (1978–84 and 1985–9), labour mobility underwent more changes in the second stage during which the economy's capacity to absorb labour was apparently greater. As compared to the change in the national structure of employment, the difference in the participation rate in

Table 4.2 Change of Labour Force by Industry in Guangdong and China, 1978–1989[6]

Year	Guangdong				China			
	Primary %	Secondary %	Tertiary %	Total (10,000)	Primary %	Secondary %	Tertiary %	Total (10,000)
(composition)								
1978	73.7	13.7	12.6	2,276	70.7	17.6	11.7	40,152
1984	63.7	18.9	17.4	2,638	64.2	20.2	15.6	48,197
1989	53.7	24.6	21.7	3,041	60.2	21.9	17.9	55,329
(average annual growth)								
1978–84	0.0	8.1	8.2	2.5	1.4	5.5	8.2	3.1
1984–89	−0.6	8.5	7.5	2.9	1.5	4.5	5.7	2.8
1978–89	−0.2	8.2	7.9	2.7	1.5	5.0	7.0	3.0

various industries is much more obvious in Guangdong than in the country as a whole, and the labour-absorbing capacity in Guangdong is higher than that at the national level. The labour shifts in Guangdong, however, are towards secondary rather than tertiary industries, which is the reverse of the national trend.[7]

THE MIGRATION OF LABOUR

Occupational mobility implies the possibility of geographical mobility. This is due partly to the liberalization of the labour market, and partly to reforms in the rural areas which allow surplus peasant labour to take up other occupations or move to other localities. Guangdong has experienced labour migration on a mass scale since 1978. In 1990, migrants in Guangdong amounted to 4.17 million. It was estimated that the migrant population clustered in the Pearl River Delta alone reached 4,000,000 in 1990 and 5,000,000 by 1991. About 80 per cent of the migrant workers in Guangdong came from within the province while the rest were of other provincial origin. By the early 1990s, there were about 1.7 million migrant workers from other provinces, the majority located in the Pearl River Delta.[8]

The ratio of migrant to local population in various cities of the Pearl River Delta is generally very high. In Shenzhen, the most distinctive 'migrant city', the migrants make up over two-thirds of the total population. The ratios for Foshan urban area and Dongguan are higher than 50 per cent. As the migrants are mostly temporary residents who cannot bring along their families, the labour participation rate of the migrant population is consequently much higher than that of the local inhabitants. The Labour Bureau of Dongguan estimated that the labour force of local origin in Dongguan had reached 730,000, while the labour force of outside origin was as high as 500,000 or 600,000. The ratio of outside *workers* to local *workers* was 68 per cent to 82 per cent in Dongguan. This is much higher than the ratio of migrant population to local population which was put at 58 per cent. It should be

Table 4.3 Migrant and Local Population of Cities and Counties in the Pearl River Delta[9]

City/County	Migrant Population (10,000)	Internal Population (10,000)	Ratio (%)
Shenzhen	165	73.2	225
Zhuhai	20	50.0	40
Dongguan	75	129.9	58
Guangzhou urban area	35	354.4	10
Foshan urban area	35	36.6	96
Shunde	20	89.9	22
Nanhai	30	89.8	33
Zhongshan	40	112.0	36
Jiangmen	50	346.0	14
Huizhou urban area	10	20.9	48
Huiyang	10	48.0	21
Huidong	8	57.1	14

noted that about half of the migrant workers in Dongguan come from other provinces (see Table 4.3).[10]

Among the migrants, 58.9 per cent migrated for business reasons, 10.6 per cent for job change or job allocation, 4.8 per cent for job training, and another 7.6 per cent to join their families.[11] The majority of the migrant population in the Pearl River Delta come from other places within the Guangdong province, and most of these 'internal' migrants come from poor and mountainous locations. For instance, it is estimated that over 200,000 workers leave Qingyuan for the more developed regions of the Pearl River Delta annually. Guangxi, Hunan, and Sichuan are the three major extra-provincial suppliers of migrant workers to Guangdong as 80 per cent of the 'external' migrants come from these three provinces.[12]

With the benefit of hindsight, it is evident that two factors in particular swelled the ranks of migrant workers in Guangdong. First, despite regular intervals of 'applied Leninism' in the urban areas, Dengist policies had brought an unprecedented emancipation and liberalization in the rural areas.

The introduction of the household production responsibility system greatly benefited certain rural areas of provinces such as Guangdong, some of which enjoyed up to three harvests annually. There was a good market in the urban and suburban areas for above-contract agricultural, horticultural, and piscicultural produce, as pre-existing levels of wealth were augmented by overseas Chinese remittances, tourism, and the cash benefits of the Hong Kong nexus.

The conditions in the 1980s enabled Cantonese in the richer parts of the province to take advantage of liberalization to increase their wealth, not only from farming but from land transactions as well. The latter took place as a result of major infrastructural development and febrile speculation about future development. For Cantonese in the less prosperous parts of the province, economic liberalization and the consequential weakening of the collective social system led to a perceptible polarization of living conditions. Those who perceived their living standards to be increasingly unsatisfactory were 'pushed' by circumstances into the ranks of migrant workers. This pressure complemented the second factor largely responsible for the changes affecting the human resources of Guangdong in this period.

This factor was the increasingly symbiotic relationship between Guangdong and Hong Kong. The 1994 Hong Kong Annual Report noted that Hong Kong accounted for two-thirds of the foreign investment in China, that Guangdong province occupied a very important position as a beneficiary of Hong Kong investment and that in Guangdong, more than three million people were working for Hong Kong companies. These were employed either in joint ventures or outward processing arrangements and compensation trade. Hong Kong thus had developed a substantial production base in Guangdong to which a significant proportion of the province's human resources was drawn in one way or another. This constituted a substantial pull factor, not only within the province but beyond its boundaries too. As the discussion of the attainment levels of human resources will show, the pull factor was both quantitative and qualitative.

Migration is legally impossible without corresponding relaxation of the household registration policy in China. Transfer of household registration is usually restricted to skilled and professional personnel employed in the province. With fast economic development, however, the inflow of migrants has become long term and continuous. This has made it necessary for the local governments to relax household registration in order to absorb the migrants as regular residents, both for the benefit of the workers and the stability of the community. For example, Shenzhen increased the quota of household transfer from 22,000 to 32,000 between 1991 and 1992. The expanded quota is however, far from able to absorb the existing 1.65 million temporary residents within the municipality.[13]

Labour migration reflects the economic development of the province, as workers generally move into the more economically developed regions within the province. Moreover, it signals the possibility of upward mobility on the part of migrants. According to a study of migrant workers, the average education level of the 'long-distant migrants' is higher than that of the 'local migrants'. This suggests that upward mobility is to some extent tied to a person's ability and education.[14]

This is illustrated by the regional distribution of graduates of all education levels within Guangdong. Table 4.4 reveals that the Pearl River Delta enjoys the lion's share of educated human resources. As shown in the table, 61.9 per cent of university graduates, 46.8 per cent of secondary specialized graduates, 94.4 per cent of senior secondary graduates, 79.9 per cent of junior secondary graduates, and 59.51 per cent of primary graduates in the province are clustered in the Pearl River Delta. While there is a high proportion of educated human resources in the delta, the proportion of the delta's teaching personnel to the province's total is not high. Considering that the population of the delta makes up only about 15 per cent of the Guangdong population,[15] it is clear that educated human resources in the province are significantly over-represented in the Pearl River Delta. Education thus has a high correlation with labour mobility.

Table 4.4 Regional Distribution of Human Resources in Guangdong, 1986 (in per cent)[16]

Regions	University Graduates	Spec. Sec. Graduates	Senior Sec. Graduates	Junior Sec. Graduates	Primary Gradutes	Teaching Personnel
Pearl River Delta	61.85	46.82	94.43	79.85	59.51	32.43
Coastal	24.60	37.17	4.16	13.29	27.33	44.22
Mountain	13.55	19.01	0.91	6.86	13.16	23.35

Table 4.5 Educational Attainment of the Guangdong
Population (in per cent)[17]

Education Levels	1964	1982	1990
Tertiary	0.38	0.48	1.5
Senior Secondary	1.48	7.92	10.3
Junior Secondary	5.14	16.89	26.5
Primary	34.86	40.63	46.6
Illiteracy/ Semi-illiteracy	30.06	16.84	15.0

THE EDUCATIONAL ATTAINMENT OF HUMAN RESOURCES

Clearly, as shown in Table 4.5, the general education level of
the Guangdong population rose significantly during the 1980s.
The increase in secondary education attainment is most obvious. In 1982, only 24.8 per cent of the population attained
secondary level of education. By 1990, the proportion had
risen to 36.8 per cent. Beyond secondary level, while the proportion of people attaining tertiary education had actually
increased by 296 per cent, the base figure was very low.[18]
Accordingly, the proportion of people with higher education is
obviously still low, making only 1.5 per cent of the Guangdong
population. Figures across regions suggest that the proportion of human resources with higher education in Guangdong
is slightly lower than the national average, and significantly
lower than Beijing and Shanghai. The Pearl River Delta has
nevertheless a large cluster of human resources with higher
education, especially in Guangzhou and Shenzhen. Even so,
they still compare unfavourably with Beijing and Shanghai
(see Table 4.6). This suggests that while there is an abundant
supply of workers available in Guangdong, there is a shortage
of technicians, managers, and professionals.

A survey on the demand for managerial personnel in the
Pearl River Delta found that in 1989, there were 8,575 middle
management positions unfilled (that is, 4 per cent of the
then optimum managerial resource base). Of these unfilled

Table 4.6 The Educational Attainment of Guangdong, China as a Whole, and the Four Asian Dragons, 1990 (per 10,000 population)[19]

Region	Higher Education Graduates	Secondary Graduates
Guangdong	134	3,197
Pearl River Delta (PRD)	267	4,037
Guangzhou	546	4,378
Shenzhen	447	6,275
Zhuhai	256	4,436
Other 5 Cities of PRD	91	3,577
Beijing	930	4,953
Shanghai	653	5,112
China (as a whole)	142	3,138
Hong Kong (1991)	891	4,029
Taiwan (1988)	1,010	4,414
South Korea (1980)	1,273	6,806

positions, 81 per cent were located in industrial enterprises, and another 12.8 per cent in wholesaling enterprises. Although a 4 per cent vacancy rate did not appear serious at first glance, further study revealed that many of the existing positions actually had been filled by under-qualified personnel. At the middle management level, 42.2 per cent of enterprises expected to employ personnel with university degrees, but only 16.7 per cent could fill their vacancies with such graduates. At the lower management level, 35.3 per cent of enterprises expected to recruit personnel with junior college qualifications, but only 23.7 per cent were able to do so. Taking the managerial population in the Pearl River Delta as a whole, the ratio of holders of post-secondary qualifications to senior secondary/specialized secondary qualifications to lower secondary qualifications was 1:4.5:4.5.[20] The evidence suggested that 90 per cent of the enterprises in the region were managed by personnel with no more than secondary education qualifications.

Other studies of the educational level of human resources

in enterprises in Guangdong show a similar picture. In one such study referring to the educational level of workers in village enterprises in the Pearl River Delta in 1991, it was reported that 76.1 per cent had attained junior secondary education, whereas only 0.56 per cent had attained tertiary education.[21] In another, referring to workers in village and town enterprises in Guangdong, 28.66 per cent attained primary education, 47.64 per cent attained junior secondary education, whereas only 0.43 per cent attained tertiary education.[22] This state of affairs has been regarded as highly unsatisfactory since it could greatly limit the development of high-tech and tertiary industries in the region.

Comparative figures also suggest that Guangdong is not yet ready to develop high-tech and tertiary industries, in terms of the educational attainment of its human resources. For example, in 1981, when the tertiary sector contributed 76 per cent of gross domestic product (GDP), the number of higher education graduates in Hong Kong was 504 per 10,000 persons. Two decades earlier in 1971, when the share of the tertiary sector was 66 per cent, the number was 282 per 10,000 persons. In comparison, the share of the higher education sector to the provincial GDP in Guangdong in 1990 was 34 per cent, while the number of higher education graduates was 134 per 10,000 persons. In Taiwan and South Korea, labour-intensive industries were still the major pillar of the economies in 1980 but they already had a proportion of higher education graduates much greater than that of neighbouring regions, for example ten times that of Guangdong's present figure. This has enabled them in recent years to push forward in developing high-tech industries. This general picture nevertheless does not entirely preclude the potential for developing high-tech and tertiary industries in Guangdong. Given that its population of 63.2 million is much bigger than any of the 'four Asian dragons', the absolute number of highly educated human resources could still be sufficient to initiate focused high-tech development.[23]

If Guangdong is to maximize the benefits of available capital and the presence of international business in Hong Kong, the provincial government and its external partners will have to commit to developing Guangdong's human resources. The comparative advantages enjoyed in the early stages of Reform and Open Door policy, notably low labour and site costs, were significantly eroded by the early 1990s. This suggests that for Guangdong to become the 'fifth dragon', the upgrading of human resources is imperative at all levels, particularly at the management level. While the educational level of human resources was clearly a major consideration for the provincial authorities, external partners were equally preoccupied with cultural considerations affecting job performance.

THE LIMITS OF CURRENT HUMAN RESOURCES

The experience of external investors in China indicates the limits of any amount of formal education up to tertiary level. Such education can only go so far in preparing the existing pool of human resources for the culture shocks of working in a foreign joint venture (JV) enterprise. Since the days of the real expatriate manager are long gone, investors have come to rely on the virtual expatriate manager from Hong Kong to manage JV enterprises. These are engaged, in particular, in outward processing and in the hotel and tourism industry. Posting a Hong Kong executive to China is not always popular for several reasons, including the disparity in home comforts, lifestyle, recreation, and support services. For these reasons, it has become necessary to subsidize substantially the salaries of virtually expatriate Hong Kong executives in Guangdong and elsewhere in China. It appears that over the long term, external investors must facilitate the training of indigenous executives in the values and practices of modern management systems.

Such management values and procedures encompass those successfully adopted or adapted in Japan, Singapore, Taiwan, and Hong Kong as well as in Western cultures. What they all have in common is that while each is culturally specific, it prepares candidates for the universal market economy. This is the direction in which indigenous executives will be encouraged to go, even though they have been nurtured in the socialist political economy where success is often influenced by clientelism and personal connections (*guanxi*) as much as by objectively measured performance.

To a large extent, therefore, the successful development of human resources at the executive level in Guangdong presents two challenges. The first, clearly demonstrated in the foregoing evidence, is the need for more people with formal tertiary education. This need is particularly acute in the key forty to fifty age group whose education was affected by the Cultural Revolution. The second is the need to train sufficient numbers of indigenous executives (those whose formal education or subsequent experience qualify them for leadership tasks), to make the transition from management in a socialist planned economy to management in a market economy.

These are formidable challenges. By meeting them, the authorities and external partners could enable Guangdong in the long run to consolidate its position as the fifth dragon. Conversely, the longer it takes to develop human resources to a level where the supply adequately matches demand, the more difficult it will be for Guangdong, for all its geographical advantages, to stay 'one step ahead' (to borrow the title of Ezra Vogel's book).[24]

THE RECRUITMENT OF HUMAN RESOURCES

There have been no lack of calls for speeding up the development of well-educated, well-trained human resources in the province.[25] An instant solution to the problem of the shortage of educated trained personnel is to recruit staff and workers elsewhere in China. Given Guangdong's booming economy and the ability to pay higher salaries and wages than other regions, this has been a popular practice. A major source of talent is university graduates or tertiary level students from other provinces, who have studied in Guangdong and been allowed to stay there on graduation. It is reported that among these extra-provincial graduates in Guangdong, some 70 per cent have been allowed to remain.[26] Regarding direct recruitment from elsewhere in China, it is reported that over 140,000 technicians and professionals were officially transferred to the province during the 1980s, while the number of those working in the province without fulfilling the official transfer process far exceeded this number.[27] In Xunde city alone, the number of personnel transferred to the city totalled 6,374, of whom 31.7 per cent were university graduates.[28]

As the urgent demand for educated and trained personnel rose, recruitment strategies of Guangdong enterprises became quite aggressive. Individual municipalities organized employers to liaise with institutions in other provinces to arrange for the assignment of university graduates. Among the inducements were the promise of various privileges including household registration (*hukou*), housing, and a cost-free move, not to mention the enhanced salary and wage arrangements. With typical Cantonese initiative and flexibility, some Guangdong enterprises developed joint ventures with established enterprises in other provinces, with the Guangdong partners providing capital and the extra-provincial counterparts providing technical personnel.[29] Of these incentives offered to qualified personnel, the Guangdong remuneration package is clearly very attractive, particularly when linked to housing. Equally, the opportunity legally or extra-legally to acquire a Guangdong *hukou* is a significant inducement since the household registration system, even in post-rationing China, remains a less effective but enforceable restraint on the free movement of population. A Guangzhou *hukou* is said to cost between 30,000 and 40,000 renminbi (RMB) on the black market, offering a useful indicator of the business opportunities perceived to exist in the province.

Another source of talent is the Guangdong students who have studied elsewhere. The evidence is that the growing material prosperity in certain parts of the province already ensures that this group, who have chosen to pursue further studies in other provinces, will return. In recent years, the majority of Guangdong students in national universities around the country, some 6,000 annually, have indicated that they wish to return to their home province on graduation.[30]

Yet another significant source of technicians, managers, and professionals are overseas Chinese students. Recently, the Guangdong government has extended preferential treatment accorded to overseas Chinese students to include free entry and exit, free choice of jobs by self-funded students, better housing, and higher wages. It is particularly noteworthy that Shenzhen sent a representative to the United States specifically for recruitment purposes, emulating a practice adopted by the Government of Hong Kong to promote its localization policy. In a similar development, Foshan has forged a linkage with Hong Kong, enabling overseas Chinese students to be employed in Hong Kong and to be sent by the Hong Kong–based companies to the municipality.[31]

THE NATIONAL SHIFT TOWARDS VOCATIONAL EDUCATION

Although investment in education and training takes effect far more slowly than recruitment from extra-provincial sources, it is the most important permanent solution to the scarcity of human resources. In addition to extending universal general education to the junior secondary level, the 1980s also witnessed what in effect was a major breakthrough in China's existing education system. For want of a better term, we shall call this 'vocationalization'. Specifically, the Chinese government appears determined to break away from the existing academic orientation of the education system by raising the ratio of vocational to non-vocational general schools at the secondary level. The direction for change was announced in a government document issued in 1980 entitled 'On the Reform of the Secondary Education Structure'. The document criticized the existing unitary structure of general secondary education, and 'suggested' that some general schools should be converted into skilled workers' schools, secondary vocational schools, and agricultural schools.[32]

In 1983, another key government document on education was issued, entitled 'Suggestions on the Reform of the Municipal Secondary Education System and the Development of

Vocational/Technical Education'. It elaborated on the need for trained human resources to speed up economic development. It also suggested that enterprises should be encouraged to offer vocational education, and set a target ratio of 50:50 between general senior secondary students and vocational students to be achieved by 1990. At the time this suggestion was made, the average prevailing ratio in the country was 5:1.[33]

In 1985, there was a new push for educational reform, marked by the publication of the 'Decision on Reform of Educational Structure'. The Decision document put forward the principle of 'training before employment', and stressed that no one, particularly those to be engaged in highly specialized and technical work, should be allowed to take up a job before receiving a certificate of qualification.[34] Furthermore, the document reiterated the ideal of achieving a 50:50 ratio between general senior secondary and vocational enrolments by 1990:

> [We] should transform a number of regular senior middle schools into vocational ones or set up vocational classes or start new schools of this type so that, within five years, enrolment in senior middle vocational and technical schools will equal that of regular senior middle schools in most places. This should put an end to the existing irrational structure of our secondary education.[35]

The 1985 document was very influential in the sense that as a 'decision' it was mandatory, in contrast to the 1983 document which was discretionary. By now, the 5:1 ratio of general secondary students to vocational students had already become 7:3.[36] In 1991, the 'Decision on the Further Development of Vocational and Technical Education' was promulgated. The effect of this decision was to specify a '3+1' model to be applied in the rural areas, that is, a one-year vocational training on top of a three-year junior secondary education.[37]

THE 'VOCATIONALIZATION' OF SECONDARY EDUCATION

Faced with an urgent need for more technicians, managers, and professionals, the decisions taken at the national level were well received by the Guangdong provincial government. As Table 4.7 shows, between 1980 and 1991, enrolments increased by approximately four times in secondary specialized schools, by 3.4 times in skilled workers' schools, and by 12 times in secondary vocational schools. They also doubled in secondary teacher-training institutes. In 1990, the enrolment ratio between general senior secondary and vocational schools had already reached 51.49.[38] In Guangdong, new secondary vocational schools emerged nearly annually. In 1991, twenty-nine senior secondary vocational schools were established, and another fourteen in 1992, many through private funding. Most of the non-governmental vocational schools are located in Guangzhou, Foshan, Zhanjiang, Maoming, and Taishan.[39]

To boost further the development of vocational and technical education, the provincial government issued a notice in 1989, entitled 'Notice on Speeding up the Development of Secondary Specialized Schools and Vocational Schools'. In addition to confirming the central policies on vocational education and training in technology, the Notice further extended schools' autonomy in administration, staffing, financing, and curricula. It also allowed schools to establish links with enterprises to offer vocational training, as well as to run business and provide consultancy services in order to 'generate income'.[40]

In the light of these liberalized and essentially more pragmatic education and training policies at the national and provincial levels, Guangdong has successfully widened the operational scope of its educational institutions. Unlike the past, when there was only the state-run school, there are now three additional types of schools:

1. those jointly run with inland institutions to offer educational and training programmes relevant to a city's development in relation to its economy and external relations;

2. those jointly run with enterprises to offer courses specifically related to needs of the business sector; and

3. those run by enterprises to offer courses specifically related to their own needs.[41]

By the mid-1990s, trials had been carried out with a '2+1' system at the senior secondary level. This system requires students to attend two years of senior secondary education, and to obtain certain passes in open certificate examinations, before being transferred to the vocational stream for vocational training in their third year of senior secondary education. This system is intended to strengthen the academic background of vocational graduates and enhance their adaptability to job shifts in the rapidly developing economy.

THE 'VOCATIONALIZATION' OF HIGHER EDUCATION

Higher education has also made significant direct contributions to the development of technical, managerial, and professional personnel in Guangdong. Resembling the practice of general secondary schools, comprehensive universities such as Zhongshan University and Shenzhen University have introduced management and technology courses. The 1980s also saw the emergence of tertiary level vocational institutes. In 1981, the Foreign Trade Institute was established. Since 1983, the pace of the establishment of higher vocational institutes has been remarkable. In that year, three such institutes were set up, namely the Guangdong Financial Institute (later renamed Guangdong Commercial Institute), Guangzhou University, and Guangdong Workers' Amateur University. In 1984, four more institutes were introduced, namely Guangdong Agricultural Management Institute for Cadres, South China Agricultural University, Guangzhou City Construction University, and Guangzhou Institute of Financial Management for Cadres. In 1985, four additional vocational universities were established, namely, Wuyi University, Jiaying University, Xijiang University, and Shaoguan University. In 1986, another two were added, namely Foshan University and Shantou University, the latter with generous financing by the Hong Kong business tycoon Li Ka-shing. The vocational universities offer short-term tertiary-level vocational training programmes, lasting from two to three years.[42]

Taking into consideration the establishment of other comprehensive universities such as Shenzhen University, the expansion rate of higher education in the 1980s in Guangdong was unprecedented. It should be noted that nearly all the universities mentioned were established with the help of private donations. In addition to the above list, other institutes established with the help of private funding include the two Teachers' Colleges of Shenzhen and Guangzhou, as well as Hainan University located in what was formerly part of Guangdong.[43] The source of private funding included successful Cantonese, Chaozhou, and Hakka business people of Guangdong origin living in Hong Kong or in the overseas Chinese diaspora. The donations reflect their commitment to the economic development of their home province.

THE VOCATIONALIZATION OF NON-FORMAL EDUCATION

Adult education offers flexible and convenient on-the-job training for a substantial number of working people in Guangdong. Enrolment in institutions of adult higher education and correspondence programmes offered by regular tertiary institutions totalled 106,128 in 1988, a seven-fold increase from 1978.[44] By 1992, 31 per cent of all employees and 45 per cent of specialized managerial cadres (*Zhuanye Guanlie Ganbu*) were enroled in some sort of continuing education course.[45]

The municipal governments and individual enterprises in the Pearl River Delta have taken positive and flexible measures to provide vocational education for the working populace within the region, and to upgrade the technical levels of their staff through external relations. For example, Shenzhen has encouraged the introduction of training programmes from outside in three ways: programmes providing for cooperation

in the development of technology; requiring foreign companies to offer staff training programmes as part of joint business
contracts; and employing overseas experts and consultants to
offer staff training.

Over the past decade, such centres and agencies as the Office
for Importing Foreign Human Resources, the Industrial and
Economic Management Training Centre, Shenzhen University, Shenzhen Adult Education Centre, and Shenzhen China
Bank have established links, to cite some examples, with the
Hong Kong Modernized Export Promotion Association, the
Hong Kong New China Human Resources Consultancy,
the Hong Kong China Bank Training Centre, and the Aus-
tralian Business Management Association, to arrange training
for Shenzhen managers, administrators, and government officials. Training programmes are not restricted to Shenzhen
and classes are also held in Hong Kong to allow administrators, managers, and key officials to be exposed to external
ideas and practices. The municipal government has also encouraged overseas Chinese and private institutions to run
schools.[46] As a more long-term strategy in the development of
human resources, it sends students to Hong Kong or overseas
to receive professional and management training. Such students are expected to collect teaching material and details of
equipments to enable them subsequently to run their own
training programmes.[47]

New models for the vocational education system have been
designed and applied on an experimental basis. Recent trends
point to the establishment of a system which offers an as-
cending hierarchy of educational qualifications, parallel to that
of the general academic stream. For example, a recent model
proposed is a primary vocational-secondary vocational-higher
vocational model, equivalent to the primary-secondary-higher
education model in the general academic stream.[48] The out-
come of these experiments is yet to be assessed, but what
seems certain is that China in general, and Guangdong in
particular, are convinced of the need for job-specific training
to meet their human resources needs. Moreover, this national
and regional conviction has exposed the need to develop a

customized, characteristically Chinese model of vocational education (see Table 4.7).[49]

ONE STEP AHEAD

This chapter has attempted to delineate how the human resource profile in Guangdong has changed in line with changing political and economic circumstances. It is evident that the effect of the reform and open door policies has been conspicuous in Guangdong in creating huge demands on human resources. There have been manifest consequential changes in the employment structure. The phasing out of life tenure and the introduction of the contract system of employment have led to substantive change in the operation of the system of supply and demand in the labour force.

Associated with the reform policies and their effect on human resources are the acceptance both of geographical mobility and occupational mobility. In these respects, the phenomenal degree of labour mobility involved in Guangdong's development could not have occurred without more flexible implementation of employment and household registration policies. Even so, the economy's growing demand for human resources remains so large that there is, inevitably, a substantial 'illegal' migrant population in the Pearl River Delta. Significant numbers are there on a temporary and indeed legally fragile basis, not having gone through the officially prescribed procedures for the transfer of household registration.

These migrants, most of whom seek factory work, are vulnerable to multifarious forms of social, political, and economic exploitation. They are part of the estimated 100 million people on the move in contemporary China. Most have abandoned agriculture because on the one hand their rural areas could not support higher living standards even given the incentives of the household-based production responsibility system or, on the other hand, because the lure of the urban lifestyle is simply too seductive.

Economic and geographical liberalization has been reflected in changes in the education system. The policy of loosening

Table 4.7 Enrolment Trends in Vocational, Secondary, and Higher Education in Guangdong, 1978–1991 (per 10,000 population)[50]

Type of School	1978	1980	1985	1990	1991
Secondary Specialized					
Schools*	1.19	1.32	1.32	1.79	1.77
Students	2.34	2.78	4.23	9.00	9.21
Graduates	0.60	0.99	1.03	2.49	2.95
Skilled Workers' Schools*	—	82	97	127	136
Students	—	1.61	1.45	5.22	5.63
Graduates	—	0.97	0.35	1.56	1.70
Secondary Vocational/					
Agricultural Schools*	—	132	345	525	550
Students	—	1.72	11.5	22.2	21.4
Graduates	—	0.38	1.35	6.68	7.12
Secondary Teacher Training					
Institutes*	96	72	46	45	46
Students	1.30	1.78	2.26	3.09	3.17
Graduates	0.49	0.79	0.69	1.00	1.08
Secondary General Schools*	2,236	2,681	3,849	3,879	3,822
Students	313.3	252.1	236.4	234.0	238.3
Graduates	109.7	66.5	53.3	71.3	70.5
Tertiary Institutes*	26	27	41	45	41
Students	3.07	4.10	6.99	9.60	9.27
Graduate	0.52	0.76	1.10	3.37	3.26

* Absolute numbers

job assignments, under which on graduation students are allocated by the authorities to work units, and which was officially approved in 1989, has had significant implications for educational establishments.[51] Shenzhen University was founded in 1983 on the principle of no job assignment. It pioneered the introduction of market mechanisms to the education sector.[52] The provision for 'mutual selection' (*shuangxiang xuanze*) between employer and employee further signifies the introduction of market supply-and-demand concepts into the education/training sector. With excessive demand for educated human resources in the growing economy, the government cannot but encourage private participation in the establishing of vocational training institutes. The fact that the major tertiary vocational training institutions are now supported by private funding confirms this need. The emergence of this type of institution clearly marks a departure from the preference for a unitary system of state educational and training institutions in China.

Our study shows that the linking of general education to enterprises has been strengthened by allowing general schools to run enterprises either on their own or jointly with other companies. This policy was adopted to allow these schools to 'generate income', to compensate for insufficient funding from government. With such shifts in the funding base, schools are now enjoying greater flexibility in educational matters and autonomy in administration.

The notion that 'education is useless' is prevalent in Guangdong in the context of rapid economic development, as people have found it faster and easier to earn money by engaging in business and seeking employment in the Pearl River Delta rather than by pursuing further studies. This study maintains, however, that education still matters for upward mobility in the job market. While employees want quick access to jobs and good wages, various surveys have shown that employers do want people with higher qualifications. This creates a market demand to which the employees will gradually respond and explains the emergence of a number of vocational universities in Guangdong.

Lastly, we have discussed the symbiotic economic relationship between Guangdong and Hong Kong. Ethnic identity as well as economic complementarity have contributed to the emergence of a relationship increasingly characterized by one integrated economy and two separate government systems. Within this increasingly integrated economy however, there is creative tension between the demands in terms of the supply of human resources of the internationally orientated Hong Kong aspects on the one hand and the domestically provisioned Guangdong aspects on the other. This tension is to some extent addressed as we noted, on the Chinese side by the substantial quantitative and qualitative shifts in the formal and informal education and training systems in Guangdong. On the Hong Kong side, there is a fairly constant impression given of gaps in the supply of human resources needed to staff the Hong Kong related local and overseas enterprises established in Guangdong.

The gaps are perceived in both management practices and job related skills. Clearly, existing measures to bridge these gaps must be augmented. While the existence of a relatively high-salary and wage-driven human resources market is desirable, its advantages can only outweigh the disadvantages when there is greater competition among job-seekers at all levels than among employers. Guangdong to some extent does suffer from a catch-22 situation, where enterprises whose business cannot further develop without better trained human resources are reluctant to invest in training, for fear their employees will be poached by competitors. In the further development of human resources in Guangdong, continuously proactive policies will be required. These will involve in particular, not only the education and training institutions in Hong Kong, but also the corporate sector and the professional associations and specialized training agencies there, to enable Guangdong to stay one step ahead and by implication, Hong Kong's continued prosperity.

AUTHORS' NOTE

This chapter is dedicated to our late and greatly lamented friend, Richard F. Goodings, of the University of Durham (UK) School of Education who devoted his life to the field of comparative education. The content of the chapter has also benefited from research generated by the project, 'Education and Manpower Development in the Pearl River Delta' funded by the University of Hong Kong committee on research and conference grants.

NOTES

1. Toyojiro Maruya, 'Guangdong as a Model of National Economic Development in China', in Edward K. Y. Chen and Toyojiro Maruya (eds.), *A Decade of 'Open-door' Economic Development in China, 1979–1989*, Hong Kong: Centre of Asian Studies, the University of Hong Kong; Tokyo: Institute of Developing Economies, 1992, pp. 153–83.

2. P. W. Liu, R. Y. C. Wong, Y. W. Sung, and P. K. Lau, *China's Economic Reform and Development Strategy of Pearl River Delta*, Hong Kong: Nanyang Commercial Bank Ltd., 1992, pp. 94–5.

3. *Guangdong in Contemporary China (Dangdai Zhongguo de Guangdong)*, Beijing: Contemporary Chinese Press, 1991, Vol. 1. Ezra F. Vogel, *One Step Ahead in China: Guangdong under Reform*, Cambridge, Mass: Harvard University Press 1989, p. 107.

4. Kong Lingyuan and Chen Siyi, 'A Study of Labour System Reform and the Development of Enterprises in Guangdong' (Guangdong Shenhua Laodong Zhidu Gaige Zengqiang Qiye Huoli de Tansuo), in Lin Ruo et al. (eds.), *Reform and Liberalisation in Guangdong (Gaige Kaifang zai Guangdong)*, Guangzhou: Guangdong Higher Education Press, 1992, pp. 165–78.

5. Maruya, 'Guangdong as Model', p. 156.

6. Ibid., p. 167.

7. Ibid., p. 168.

8. Zhou Danan, 'An Analysis of the Distribution and Trend of Migration of the Migrant Workers in the Pearl River Delta [Zhujiang Sanjiaozhou Wailai Laodong Renkou Fenbu Tezheng ji Yidong Qushi Fenxi]', in Zhongshan University Research Centre of Pearl River Delta Economic Development and Management (ed.), *Economic Development of the Pearl River Delta: A Retrospect and Prospects (Zhujiang Sanjiaozhou Jingji Fazhan Huigu yu Qianzhan)*, Guangzhou: Zhongshan University Press, 1993, pp. 271–7. Also see Guangdong Statistics Bureau, *Guangdong Statistical Yearbook, 1991*, Guangzhou: China Statistics Press, 1991, p. 113.

9. Liu et al., *China's Economic Reform*, p. 82.

10. Ibid., pp. 82–3.
11. *Guangdong Statistical Yearbook, 1991*, p. 132.
12. Liu et al., *China's Economic Reform*, p. 84.
13. Ibid., pp. 97–8.
14. Li Si-ming, 'Labour Mobility, Migration and Urbanisation in the Pearl River Delta Area', *Asian Geographer*, 8, 1 & 2 (1992): 55.
15. Lo Chor Pang, 'Population Change and Urban Development in the Pearl River Delta: Spatial Policy Implications', *Asian Geographer*, 8, 1 & 2 (1989): p. 17.
16. *Guangdong Higher Education (Guangdong Gaodeng Jiaoyu)*, Guangzhou: Guangdong Education Press, 1989. Guangdong Human Resources Studies Centre, 'A Re-examination of and Reflection on Guangdong's Human Resources in Science and Technology' (Guangdong Keji Rencai Taishi de Zairenshi yu Ruogan Sikao). Paper presented at the Fourth Symposium on Theories and Policies of the Guangdong Reform Experiment District (Guangdong Gaige Shiyanqu Lilun yu Duice disi Zhuanti Yantaohui), Guangzhou, 1988.
17. *Guangdong in Contemporary China*, p. 221.
18. Population Census Office, Guangdong Province (ed.), *Tabulation on the 1990 Population Census of Guangdong Province*, Guangdong: China Statistical Publishing House, 1992.
19. Liu et al, *China's Economic Reform*, p. 88 and Zhou Danan, 'An Analysis of the Distribution and Trend of Migration of Migrant Workers', Table 3.2.
20. Chen Zhenxiong and Zheng Zongcheng, *The Need for Training Enterprises Managerial Personnel in the Pearl River Delta (Zhujiang Sanjiaozhou Qiye Renyuan Renli ji Peixun Xuqiu)*. Report of the Study Group on the Need for the Enterprises Managerial Personnel, School of Management, Zhongshan University, Guangzhou: Zhongshan University Press, 1990.
21. Chen Wenxue, 'Rely on Advanced Science and Technology to Create New Strength: Questions and Reflections on the Development Village and Township Industries in the Pearl River Delta' (Yikao Keji Jinbu, Zaizao Xinyoushi: Zhujiang Sanjiaozhou Xiangzhen Gongye Fazhan Wenti yu Sikao), in Zhongshan University Research Centre of Pearl River Delta Economic Development and Management (ed.), *Economic Development of the Pearl River Delta: A Retrospect and Prospects (Zhujiang Sanjiaozhou Jingji Fazhan Huigu yu Qianzhan)*, Guangzhou: Zhongshan University Press, 1993, pp. 246–53.
22. Study Group on Human Resources of Enterprises in Guangdong, 'Deepening Reform in Higher Education according to Market Mechanism—A Comprehensive Analysis of Human Resources of Enterprises in Guangdong' (Genju Shichang Tedian, Shenhua Gaodeng Jiaoyu Gaige—Guangdongsheng Xiangzhen Qiye Rencai Qingkuang Zonghe Fenxi), in Huang Jiaqu, Yan Zexian, and Feng Zengjin (eds.), *Education in the*

Pearl River Delta in the Tide of Reform (Gaige Dachaozhong de Zhujian Sanjiao Zhou Jiaoyu), Guangzhou: Guangdong Higher Education Press, 1993, pp. 48–63.

23. Liu et al, *China's Economic Reform*, pp. 89–90.

24. The data on which the authors' views are based is drawn from issues of *Business China* published by the Economist Intelligance Unit 1992–94, and the *South China Morning Post*, 24 May 1993.

25. Feng Zengjin, 'Education in the Pearl River Delta: Challenges and Development Strategies' (Zhujiang Sanjiaozhou Jiaoyu Miannin de Tiaozhan jiqi Fazhan Celue), in *Directions of Education (Jiaoyu Daokan)*, 10 (1993): pp. 36–9; Liang Ying, 'An Analysis of the Science and Technology Workforce and a Reflection on the Need for Human Resources in Guangdong' (Guangdong Keji Duiwu de Fenxi ji dui Rencai Xuqiu di Sikao) in Li Xiuhong, Zhou Heming, and Gao Guibiao (eds.), *Studies of the Education Environment and Development Strategies of Guangdong [Guangdong Jiaoyu Huanjing yu Fazhan Zhanlue Yanjiu]*, Guangzhou: Guangdong Higher Education Press, 1992, pp. 36–47.

26. Stanley Rosen, 'Student Enrolment and Job Assignment Issues', *China News Analysis*, 15 March 1993, pp. 1–9.

27. *Yangcheng Wanbao*, Guangzhou, 6 October 1993.

28. Ibid., 2 December 1993.

29. Liu et al., *China's Economic Reform*, p. 86.

30. Rosen, 'Student Enrolment and Job Assignment Issues', see note 26, p. 4.

31. Liu et al., *China's Economic Reform*, p. 86.

32. State Education Commission (Guojia Jiaoyu Weiyuan Hui) (ed.), *Selections of Significant Education Documents since the Third Plenum of the CPC Eleventh Central Committee (Shiyijie Sanzhong Quanhui Yilai Zhongyao Jiaoyu Wenxian Xuanbian)*, Beijing: Educational Science Press, 1992, pp. 58–9.

33. Ibid., pp. 128–9.

34. 'Decision of the CPC Central Committee on the Reform of China's Educational Structure, 27 May 1985', Beijing: Foreign Languages Press, 1985, p. 10; 'Decision on Further Development of Vocational and and Technical Education (Guanyu Dali Fazhan Zhiyejishu Jiaoyu de Jueding), 17 October 1991', in State Education Commission (ed.), *Selections of Significant Education Documents since the Eleventh Third Plenum (Shiyijie Sanzhong Quanhui Yilai Zhongyao Jiaoyu Wenxian Xuanbian)*, Beijing: Educational Science Press, 1992.

35. Ibid., p. 11.

36. Cheng Kai Ming, *China's Education Reform: Progress, Constraints and Tendencies* (Zhongguo Jiaoyu Gaige: Jinzhan, Juxian, Qushi), Hong Kong: Commercial Press, 1992, p. 15.

37. State Education Commission, *Selection of Significant Education Documents*, p. 516.

38. Lo Yunzhu and He Boyong, 'Preliminary Thoughts on Reform in Guangdong's Vocational and Technical Education' (Guangdong Zhiyejishu Jiaoyu Gaige de Chubu Shexiang), in Li Xiuhong, Zhou Heming, and Gao Guibiao (eds.), *Studies of the Education Environment and Development Strategies of Guangdong (Guangdong Jiaoyu Huanjing yu Fazhan Zhanlue Yanjiu)*, Guangzhou: Guangdong Higher Education Press, 1992, p. 349.

39. *Guangdong Yearbook (1992 and 1993)*, Guangzhou: Guangdong Yearbook Press, 1992, 1993.

40. Xu Xueqiang, Liang Ying, and Huang Xunluo, *Objectives and Policies: Basic Thoughts on Reform and Development in Guangdong's Higher Education (Mubian, Duice: Guangdong Gaodeng Jiaoyu Gaige yu Fazhan Jiben Silu)*, Guangzhou: Guangdong Higher Education Press, 1993, p. 106.

41. W. O. Lee and G. A. Postiglione, 'The "Window Effects" on Education and Development in South China', *CUHK Education Journal*, 21, 2 and 22, 1 (1994).

42. *Guangdong Higher Education*, p. 452.

43. *Guangdong in Contemporary China, (Dangdai Zhongguo de Guangdong)*, Vol. 2, Beijing: Contemporary Chinese Press, 1991, p. 235.

44. Grace C. L. Mak, 'Education', in Y. M. Yeung and David K. Y. Chu (eds.), *Guangdong: Survey of a Province Undergoing Rapid Change*, Hong Kong: The Chinese University Press, 1994, p. 224.

45. *Guangdong Yearbook 1993*.

46. Shenzhen Educational Science Research Institute (SESRI) (Shenzhen Jiaoy Kexue Yanjiusuo) (ed.), *A Study of the Strategies of Educational Development in Shenzhen (Shenzhenshi Jiaoyu Fazhan Zhanlue Yanjiu)*, Guangzhou: Guangdong Education Press, 1991, pp. 168–9.

47. Chen Zhixing, 'An Exploration of Importing Training' (Yinjin Peixun Chutan), in Shenzhen Education Science Research Centre (ed.), *Studies of Education in the Shenzhen Special Economic Zone (Shenzhen Tequ Jiaoyu Yanjiu)*, Wuhan: Wuhan University Press, 1985, pp. 224–6.

48. Lo and He, 'Preliminary Thoughts on Reform', p. 352.

49. Song Xiangzhong et al., *The Developing Vocational Education in Shenzhen (Fazhanzhong de Shenzhen Zhiye Jiaoyu)*, Shenzhen: Shenzhen Education Bureau, 1992, p. 3.

50. Guangdong Statistics Bureau, *Guangdong Statistical Yearbook*, Guangdong Statistics Press, 1992, Table 15–3.

51. Stanley Rosen, 'Student Enrolment', pp. 1–9.

52. W. O. Lee, 'Pressure for Educational Excellence in China: Implications for Hong Kong', in G. A. Postiglione with Y. M. Leung (eds.), *Education and Society in Hong Kong: Toward One Country and Two Systems*, New York: M. E. Sharpe, 1991, pp. 235–52.

5 THE FIFTH DRAGON: ECONOMIC DEVELOPMENT

Y. Y. Kueh and Robert F. Ash

Guangdong's economic aspiration is to catch up with the 'four dragons' of East Asia within fifteen to twenty years.[1] Many theoretical simulations purport to show how export promotion or other strategies might enable the province to achieve this goal and attain the income and consumption standards prevailing in these regions. Such exercises may vary in econometric sophistication, but they share a bullish confidence based on accelerated economic growth in the province since the early 1980s.

It is true that in recent years, Guangdong has outpaced virtually every other province in almost every aspect of economic performance. Many factors have contributed to this achievement. Foremost among them is the preferential treatment accorded by the central government since 1980, which has enabled the provincial authorities to retain fiscal revenue and foreign currency receipts in excess of obligatory—and fixed—remittances to the centre. This marks a sharp departure from previous confiscatory practices.[2]

Such financial privileges have enhanced provincial autonomy in the allocation of resources, especially in the foreign trade sector. But Guangdong's heightened economic independence has not only strengthened allocative efficiency within the province. It has also facilitated its increased integration into the world economy, paving the way for its competitive involvement in export and import markets and generating improvements in productivity in indigenous manufacturing.

The role of the Special Economic Zones (SEZ) is an important dimension of Guangdong's economic success. Three of the four original SEZs were located in the province[3] and, at least until 1988, these absorbed almost all foreign direct investment (FDI) into China—most of it coming from neighbouring Hong Kong. Such inflows of FDI have brought in their wake fundamental changes in business attitudes and practices in Guangdong and increasingly have acted as a catalyst in initiating structural changes in its economic system.

Such are the bare bones of recent economic development in Guangdong. In what follows, we seek to highlight the salient aspects of this process against the background of institutional and policy adjustments since the early 1980s. After considering the economic significance of Guangdong *vis-à-vis* China and the four East Asian dragons, we will analyze the nature and impact of economic growth and structural change both within the province itself and relative to the country as a whole. We will also look at the roles of investment and foreign capital, foreign trade, and Guangdong's links with Hong Kong. Finally, we will briefly assess the future prospects for the aspiring fifth little dragon.

THE ECONOMIC SIGNIFICANCE OF GUANGDONG PROVINCE

With a population of 65 million in 1992, Guangdong is the fifth-largest province in China, accounting for 5.5 per cent of the national total. It is also one of the most densely populated provinces, its surface area of 0.18 million square kilometres constituting a mere 1.9 per cent of the national figure.

Table 5.1 shows that in terms of its population and land base, Guangdong is a much larger entity than the four East Asian dragons.[4] But the *economic* gap between Guangdong and the other regions remains very wide.[5] Unadjusted estimates of per capita gross domestic product (GDP) show the province lagging far behind—a finding which is not materially altered

GDP/Capita

| | China | | | Four Little Dragons | | | |
| | National | GD | Ratio (9)/(8) | Hong Kong | S. Korea | Singapore | Taiwan |
	(8)	(9)	(10)	(11)	(12)	(13)	(14)
1985	11.37	18.36	1.61	-0.9	5.88	-2.79	4.1
1986	6.90	9.72	1.41	9.7	11.41	0.66	11.3
1987	9.33	15.91	1.71	13.4	10.92	8.61	10.7
1988	9.52	13.73	1.44	7.4	10.42	9.47	6.6
1989	2.71	5.25	1.94	1.8	5.18	7.61	6.2
1990	2.39	8.44	3.53	2.9	7.88	8.34	3.9
1991	6.54	14.32	2.19	3.2	7.53	4.00	6.1
1992	11.82	19.94	1.69	4.2	3.80	3.62	5.1
1979–85	7.92	10.30	1.30	4.79	5.16	5.82	5.46
1986–92	6.97	12.39	1.78	6.02	8.13	5.99	7.08
1979–92	7.44	11.34	1.52	5.40	6.63	5.90	6.27

Notes: All figures are based either on comparable prices (in the case of China and Guangdong), or constant prices—S. Korea and Singapore (1985 as base); Hong Kong, (1980); and Taiwan (1986). Column 14 refers to GNP rather than GDP.

Sources: Columns 1 and 8: *ZGTJNJ 1993*, pp. 31–32 and 81.
Columns 2 and 9: *GDTJNJ 1991*, pp. 48 and 57; *1993*, p. 79; *QJZDGD 1949–88*, pp. 44 and 54.
Columns 4 and 11: *H.K. Annual Digest of Statistics 1988*, p. 109; *1991*, p. 109; and *1993*, p. 109.
Columns 5, 6, 12, and 13: United Nations: *Statistical Yearbook for Asia and the Pacific 1990*, pp. 371–2 and 210–11; IMF, *International Financial Statistics* Nov. 1993, pp. 326 and 472.
Columns 7 and 14: *Taiwan Statistical Data Book 1993*, pp. 25 and 30.

underline the province's strong momentum of growth. During the post-1978 reform period, Guangdong's economic growth easily outpaced that of China (13.28 and 8.97 per cent per annum, respectively, between 1979 and 1992). But it also exceeded—and by an even greater margin—that of South Korea, Taiwan, Hong Kong, and Singapore.

If estimates for the more recent period offer a more appropriate basis for comparison, they also provide no less telling evidence of Guangdong's remarkable growth record.[10] For example, its annual GDP grew by 15 per cent between 1986 and 1992, compared with 9 per cent in South Korea and 8 per cent in Taiwan. Such data provide a *prima facie* case in favour of the ability of the province eventually to catch up with its Asia Pacific rivals.

The most striking indication in Table 5.3 is the acceleration of GDP growth (total and per capita) in Guangdong between 1979 and 1985, and 1986 and 1992.[11] Although this pattern of growth mirrored that of the four dragons, it was a remarkable achievement given the economic retrenchment and *deceleration* which were taking place nationally.

Several factors contributed to the contrasting provincial and national economic performances. Perhaps most important was the foundation for sustained growth and the exploitation of scale economies which had been laid in Guangdong during the first half of the 1980s and which facilitated subsequent economic expansion. The role of foreign direct investment (FDI) was critical in this respect, Guangdong being the single largest recipient of such capital inflows.[12] Many of the investment projects initiated at this time did not reach maturity until after the mid-1980s. Thus, as FDI continued to flow into the province, output growth accelerated.

By contrast, a different pattern emerged elsewhere in China. The initial net impact of early post-1978 reforms was beneficial throughout the country. But in the absence of substantial inflows of FDI, such as characterized the experience of Guangdong and other coastal regions, the effect in many interior provinces was not lasting and the boost to economic expansion given by the early reforms weakened during the second half of the 1980s.

Guangdong's spectacular performance cannot, however, simply be attributed to the *financial* impact of FDI. Through access to new technology and modern production techniques which it has also provided, FDI has been a vehicle for improvements in the managerial efficiency and competitiveness of domestic enterprises. From such sources have come the allocative realignments and rationalization mentioned earlier.

These remarks highlight the extent to which productivity improvements have increasingly become the engine of economic growth in Guangdong. As Table 5.4 shows, they also set the provincial experience apart from that of the country as a whole, where physical increases in inputs have continued to be the major source of growth.

During the Maoist era, the contribution of productivity improvements to net material product growth in Guangdong shows a sharply declining trend, reaching a mere 21 per cent during the Cultural Revolution decade (1966–76). Against this background, to have raised this figure to 49 per cent (1977–85) and 53 per cent (1986–92) is an outstanding achievement. It is all the more striking when compared with the corresponding national figures, which show a *fall* in the productivity contribution to net material product growth from 43 to 32 per cent between 1977 and 1985, and 1986 and 1992.

The role of physical capital formation in recent economic growth offers another interesting contrast. In Guangdong, the contribution of increases in capital to net material product growth declined from 37 to 34 per cent between 1977 and 1985, and 1986 and 1992, whereas nationally it rose from 38 to 51 per cent. Such estimates suggest that in much of China, in the absence of any significant productivity improvement, the growth momentum has only been maintained through increasing dependence on the physical expansion of the capital base.

At the same time, both national and provincial estimates in Table 5.4 indicate that the contribution of *labour* to income growth has consistently been in decline since the late 1950s.[13]

Table 5.4 Sources of Net Material Product (NMP) Growth in China and Guangdong Compared, 1953–1992 (in per cent)

	Growth of NMP			Labour			Contribution to NMP Growth					
							Capital			Productivity		
	National	GD	Ratio (3)/(2)	National	GD	Ratio (5)/(4)	National	GD	Ratio (8)/(7)	National	GD	Ratio (11)/(10)
	(1)	(2)	(3)	(4)	(5)	(6)	(7)	(8)	(9)	(10)	(11)	(12)
1952–57	6.61	9.05	1.369	1.67 (25.26)	2.33 (25.75)	1.395	0.84 (12.71)	0.64 (7.07)	0.762	4.10 (62.03)	6.08 (67.18)	1.483
1957–65	2.09	3.43	1.641	1.63 (77.99)	0.47 (13.70)	0.288	1.87 (89.47)	1.35 (39.36)	0.722	-1.41 (-67.46)	1.61 (46.94)	-1.142
1965–76	5.11	4.36	0.853	1.68 (32.84)	1.62 (37.16)	0.965	2.81 (54.99)	1.83 (41.97)	0.651	0.62 (12.17)	0.91 (20.87)	1.463
1977–85	8.78	10.25	1.167	1.69 (19.25)	1.48 (14.44)	0.876	3.30 (37.59)	3.77 (36.78)	1.142	3.79 (43.16)	5.00 (48.78)	1.319
1985–92	8.75	14.75	1.686	1.52 (17.37)	1.82 (12.34)	1.197	4.47 (51.09)	5.06 (34.31)	1.132	2.76 (31.54)	7.87 (53.35)	2.851

Notes: Net Material Product (NMP) and Capital are deflated figures in 1980 prices obtained by using the methodology of D. H. Perkins, as explained in his 'Reforming China's economic system', *Journal of Economic Literature*, Vol. 26 No. 2 (June 1988), pp. 628–9; except for Guangdong's capital figures which are given in comparable prices.
Labour force is year-end figures.
Figures in parentheses are percentage shares in the contribution to NMP growth.

Sources: Columns 1,4, 7, and 10: Perkins, ibid, for 1952–85, and *ZGTJNJ* 1993, pp. 33–5, 48, and 97 for 1985–92.
Columns 2, 5, 8, and 11: *GDTJNJ* 1991, pp. 115; 1993, pp. 76, 82, and 129; *Guangdong Sheng Guomin Jingji he Shehui Fazhan Tongji Ziliao: Section on Balance Statistics*, pp. 1–2, 19–20, 25–26, 31–32, and 53–54.

This finding highlights the move away from traditional sources of output expansion, as an increasingly capital-intensive process of industrialization has taken place.

The accelerated growth, at a very high level, of *per capita* GDP growth is another noteworthy aspect of Guangdong's recent economic performance. Average per capita growth rose from 10 to 12 per cent per annum between 1979 and 1985, and 1986 and 1992, whilst the corresponding national figure fell from 8 to 7 per cent.[14] What is more, this buoyant performance was accompanied by an above-average expansion of population (see Table 5.2). This is the background to a demographic phenomenon which has attracted much attention in recent years: namely, the migration of large numbers of people from all parts of China in search of employment in Guangdong.

In short, far from adhering to the image of a labour-surplus economy, Guangdong has now begun to display the attributes of labour *shortage*. In making this transformation, it has distanced itself from the rest of China, where surplus labour conditions persist, and followed the path of the other East Asian dragons.

STRUCTURAL CHANGES IN INCOME AND EMPLOYMENT

Empirical evidence suggests a strong correlation between rapid income growth, accelerated industrialization, and structural economic change. The figures in Tables 5.5 and 5.6 seek to highlight these changes, as they have taken place in Guangdong and China as a whole.

Both the national and provincial estimates show that under the impact of new economic priorities emerging out of the Third Plenum of the 11th CCP Central Committee (December 1978), the contribution of agriculture to GDP increased between 1978 and 1982. Thereafter, this trend was reversed— but much more sharply in Guangdong (from 36 to 20 per cent between 1982 and 1992) than in the rest of the country (from 34 to 24 per cent). The contraction in the agricultural

Table 5.5 Contrasting Changes in GDP Structure in China and Guangdong 1978–1992 (in per cent)

	Agriculture			Industry			Services		
	National	GD	Ratio (2)/(1)	National	GD	Ratio (5)/(4)	National	GD	Ratio (8)/(7)
	(1)	(2)	(3)	(4)	(5)	(6)	(7)	(8)	(9)
1978	28.4	29.9	1.05	48.6	46.4	0.95	23.0	23.7	1.03
1979	31.5	32.2	1.02	47.9	43.8	0.91	20.6	24.0	1.17
1980	30.4	33.8	1.11	49.0	41.1	0.84	20.6	25.1	1.22
1981	32.4	33.2	1.02	47.2	41.7	0.88	20.4	25.1	1.23
1982	34.0	35.7	1.05	46.0	40.2	0.87	20.0	24.1	1.21
1983	33.9	33.9	1.00	45.7	41.9	0.92	20.4	24.2	1.19
1984	33.1	32.9	0.99	44.8	41.6	0.93	22.1	25.5	1.15
1985	29.8	31.1	1.04	45.3	40.8	0.90	24.9	28.1	1.13
1986	28.5	29.6	1.04	46.4	39.0	0.84	25.1	31.4	1.25

1987	28.3	28.8	1.02	46.5	39.4	0.85	25.2	31.8	1.26
1988	27.2	27.9	1.03	46.8	40.4	0.86	26.0	31.7	1.22
1989	26.4	26.8	1.02	45.5	40.3	0.89	28.1	32.9	1.17
1990	28.4	26.1	0.92	43.7	39.9	0.91	27.9	34.0	1.22
1991	26.2	23.4	0.89	45.2	42.1	0.93	28.6	34.5	1.21
1992	23.9	20.3	0.85	48.2	45.9	0.95	27.9	33.8	1.21
Average:									
1978–85	31.8	32.9	1.03	46.5	41.8	0.90	21.7	25.3	1.17
1986–92	26.6	24.9	0.94	46.0	41.8	0.91	27.4	33.3	1.22

Sources: Columns 1, 4, and 7: *ZGTJNJ 1993*, pp. 31–2.
Columns 2, 5, and 8: *GDTJNJ 1991*, p. 57; *1993*, pp. 77–9; and *QJZDGD 1949–88*, p. 54.

share reflected a major expansion in those of both industry and services. This pattern is common to both Guangdong and China, although since 1982 it has been more pronounced in the former. The rapid expansion of the service sector is another striking feature of structural change in Guangdong throughout the post-1978 reform period.

The changing structure of *employment* during the same period is illustrated in Table 5.6.

The general trends apply at both the national and provincial level, although changes in the distribution of the labour force between the major sectors have been more pronounced in Guangdong. Thus, the percentage decline in agricultural employment in favour of increases in industry and services has been sharper in Guangdong than in China as a whole.[15] Suffice to say that the structural changes revealed in Tables 5.5 and 5.6 are similar to those which took place in South Korea, Taiwan, Hong Kong, and Singapore at comparable periods in their economic development.[16]

The real significance of these trends is, however, in their implications for productivity. Table 5.7 presents estimates of relative product per worker in agriculture, industry, and services in Guangdong and all of China. It provides convincing evidence of converging trends in labour productivity between the three sectors.

The more rapid growth in relative product per agricultural worker in Guangdong no doubt reflects accelerated outflows of labour from farming into industry and services—a process which helped mitigate labour pressures associated with provincial economic development.[17] These transfers dampened potential rises in per worker *income* in non-agricultural sectors of the province. They also exerted an equalizing influence on relative product per worker within all three sectors.

This finding is underlined by the estimates of total inequality shown in Table 5.7. They show a consistent decline in provincial inequality from 0.88 (1978) to 0.58 (1985) to 0.53 (1992). The corresponding figures for China (0.84, 0.65, and 0.69) also reflect a decline after 1978, but one which was not as sharp, nor as consistent. The convergence in sectoral

Changes in employment structure in China and Guangdong, 1978–1992 (in per cent)

	Agriculture			Industry			Services		
	National	GD	Ratio (2)/(1)	National	GD	Ratio (5)/(4)	National	GD	Ratio (8)/(7)
	(1)	(2)	(3)	(4)	(5)	(6)	(7)	(8)	(9)
1978	70.5	73.68	1.05	17.4	13.75	0.79	12.1	12.57	1.04
1979	69.8	71.98	1.03	17.7	16.53	0.93	12.5	11.49	0.92
1980	68.7	70.68	1.03	18.3	17.10	0.93	13.0	12.22	0.94
1981	68.1	70.13	1.03	18.4	16.91	0.92	13.5	12.96	0.96
1982	68.1	68.35	1.00	18.5	17.74	0.96	13.4	13.91	1.04
1983	67.1	67.30	1.00	18.8	17.85	0.95	14.1	14.85	1.05
1984	64.0	63.68	0.99	20.0	18.89	0.94	16.0	17.43	1.09
1985	62.4	60.14	0.96	20.9	21.14	1.01	16.7	18.72	1.12
1986	60.9	57.76	0.95	21.9	22.68	1.04	17.2	19.56	1.14
1987	59.9	55.14	0.92	22.3	24.19	1.08	17.8	20.67	1.16
1988	59.3	53.66	0.90	22.4	24.84	1.11	18.3	21.50	1.17
1989	60.0	53.67	0.89	21.7	24.59	1.13	18.3	21.74	1.19
1990	60.0	52.97	0.88	21.4	27.21	1.27	18.6	19.82	1.07
1991	59.8	50.48	0.84	21.4	28.62	1.34	18.8	20.90	1.11
1992	58.5	47.35	0.81	21.7	30.44	1.40	19.8	22.21	1.12
Average:									
1978–85	67.16	68.01	1.01	18.79	17.79	0.95	14.05	14.20	1.01
1986–92	59.72	52.83	0.88	21.83	26.23	1.20	18.45	20.94	1.13

Sources: Columns 1, 4, and 7: ZGTJNJ 1993, p. 101,
Columns 2, 5, and 8: GDTJNJ 1989, p. 87; 1991, p. 115; 1993, p. 129.

Table 5.7 Changes in Relative Product per Worker for Agricultural, Industrial, and Services Sectors, and Total Inequality among Sectors in China, and Guangdong, selected years 1978–1992

1978	Relative Product per Worker		
	National (1)	**GDP** (2)	**Ratio(2)/(1)** (3)
Agriculture	0.40	0.41	1.01
Industry	2.79	3.37	1.21
Services	1.90	1.89	0.99
1985			
Agriculture	0.48	0.52	1.08
Industry	2.17	1.93	0.89
Services	1.49	1.50	1.01
1992			
Agriculture	0.41	0.43	1.06
Industry	2.22	1.51	0.68
Services	1.49	1.50	1.01
	Total Inequality		
	National (4)	**GD** (5)	**Ratio(5)/(4)** (6)
1978	0.84	0.88	1.04
1985	0.65	0.58	0.89
1992	0.69	0.53	0.77

Notes: Relative Product per Worker = (% share in GDP)/(% share in Employment). Total inequality = $\Sigma[1 - Y(i)]$. $W(i)$; $Y(i)$ = relative product per worker at sector i; $W(i)$ = percentage share in employment of sector i.

Sources: See Tables 5.5 and 5.6.

productivity in Guangdong during the reform era is likely to be unprecedented anywhere else in China since 1949.

INVESTMENT AND THE ROLE OF FOREIGN CAPITAL

Estimates presented in the previous section showed that in Guangdong after 1978, the declining contribution to income (net material product) growth of physical increases in capital and labour was offset by higher factor productivity (that is, improved input efficiency). That the annual average rate of net material product growth in Guangdong rose from 10 per cent (1977–85) to 15 per cent (1986–92) illustrates the impact of such productivity improvements.

Attempting to identify and measure the sources of productivity growth is notoriously difficult.[18] In Guangdong's case, apart from technological progress embodied in imported hardware, the list would surely include improvements in workers' incentives and in managerial know-how associated with the establishment of Sino-foreign joint ventures. Dynamic forces arising out of increased competition in international markets and growing marketization of the domestic economy have also generated a more rational pattern of inter-provincial specialization, and so of resource allocation, within the province. It is true that all these factors have also been at work elsewhere in China, especially in the coastal regions. But more than any other region of the country, Guangdong has come to epitomize the dynamism inherent in post-1978 reforms.

Table 5.8 highlights the role of capital—especially foreign investment—in the buoyant economic performance of Guangdong.

The estimates show that just as Guangdong's GDP growth exceeded the national average, so too did the expansion of fixed capital formation. As a result, the province's share in national fixed investment increased almost three-fold, from 4.2 per cent (1980) to 11.7 per cent (1992). The inference is that favourable incentives and investment opportunities encouraged the re-investment of profits and tax revenue, thereby sustaining the continued expansion of the capital stock.

An interesting aspect of this process has been the active involvement of the state-owned sector in Guangdong. Between 1979 and 1985, and 1986 and 1992, this sector's average share in gross investment increased from 65 to 72 per cent, compared with a corresponding *decline* (from 68 to 65 per cent) in China as a whole. This finding is at first glance surprising. It is, after

Table 5.8 Fixed Investment Expenditure in China and Guangdong: Growth Rates and Share of the State-owned Sector Compared, 1978–1992

	Gross Investment (100 million yuan)			Growth Rates (%)			Share of Stated-owned Sector (%)		
	National	GD	Ratio (%) (2)/(1)	National	GD	Ratio (5)/(4)	National	GD	Ratio (8)/(7)
	(1)	(2)	(3)	(4)	(5)	(6)	(7)	(8)	(9)
1978	—	27.23	—	—	—	—	—	73.60	—
1979	—	28.29	—	—	3.89	—	—	70.91	—
1980	910.85	38.29	4.20	—	35.35	—	81.89	67.17	0.82
1981	961.00	60.40	6.29	5.51	57.74	10.49	69.46	57.30	0.82
1982	1,230.40	84.73	6.89	28.03	40.28	1.44	68.70	61.10	0.89
1983	1,430.10	88.71	6.20	16.23	4.70	0.29	66.57	63.04	0.95
1984	1,832.90	130.37	7.11	28.17	46.96	1.67	64.66	61.86	0.96
1985	2,543.20	184.59	7.26	38.75	41.59	1.07	66.08	71.03	1.07
1986	3,019.60	216.50	7.17	18.73	17.29	0.92	65.52	73.25	1.12
1987	3,640.90	251.01	6.89	20.58	15.94	0.77	63.12	71.30	1.13

1988	4,496.50	353.59	7.86	23.50	40.87	1.74	61.44	71.90	1.17
1989	4,137.70	347.34	8.39	-7.89	-1.77	0.22	61.28	72.89	1.19
1990	4,449.30	372.59	8.37	7.53	7.27	0.97	65.60	73.05	1.11
1991	5,508.80	478.20	8.68	23.81	28.34	1.19	65.86	71.73	1.09
1992	7,854.98	921.75	11.73	42.59	92.75	2.18	67.14	65.45	0.97
Average:									
1978–85	1,484.74	80.33	5.41	22.80	31.44	1.38	68.21	65.34	0.96
1986–92	4,729.68	420.14	8.88	17.48	25.83	1.48	64.62	71.50	1.11

Notes: Figures for yuan are all in current prices, and gross investment refers to 'total fixed assets investment of the whole society' covering investment made by different ownership sectors including Sino-foreign joint ventures and private/collective undertakings.

Sources: Columns 1, 4, and 7: ZGTJNJ 1991, p. 143; 1993, p. 145; and Zhongguo Guding Zichan Touzi Tongji Ziliao 1950–85 (Statistical Materials on Fixed Assets Investment in China 1950–85), p. 5.
Columns 2, 5, and 8: GDTJNJ 1993, p. 236.

all, at variance with the familiar perception of Guangdong as a region in which heavy industries have been in decline and the state sector has contracted in favour of expanded private and collective economic activities. The state sector's continued strength derives in fact from two major factors. One is the provincial government's increased investment in large-scale infrastructural projects (construction of road and rail links, port facilities; installation of sophisticated telecommunications networks in order to accommodate burgeoning industrial and commercial activities). The other is the fact that most Sino–foreign joint venture investment projects in the province have been undertaken with the participation of state enterprises.

Guangdong has been the largest single recipient of foreign capital (especially foreign direct investment) in China. Between 1985 and 1992, on average, it absorbed 22 per cent of all foreign capital entering the country (including borrowing from overseas governments and financial institutions), and 34 per cent of total realized FDI (see Table 5.9). It is noteworthy that in the wake of Deng Xiaoping's 'southern tour' (*nanxun*) during January and February 1992, the rate of growth of both total foreign capital and FDI inflows accelerated sharply in 1992 and 1993.[19] However, the decline (from 42 to 32 per cent) in Guangdong's share of national FDI in 1992 suggests that the predicted dispersal of foreign investment from South China along the coast to East and North China may now have started to take place.[20]

The national preeminence of Guangdong as a recipient of foreign capital itself suggests the significance of such resource flows in financing gross capital formation in the province. The estimates in Tables 5.8 and 5.9 indicate that in recent years FDI contributed more than 20 per cent of provincial gross capital formation.[21] Even more telling is the finding that every US dollar of foreign investment has required the expenditure of some 3 yuan in complementary investment.[22] Such calculations leave no room for doubt that the growth of fixed asset investment in Guangdong has been closely related to the expansion of foreign investment.

We have already indicated that increased supplies of capital contributed around 34 per cent of average provincial net material product growth of 15 per cent per annum during 1986 to 1992 (Table 5.4). Set in this context, the 30 per cent share of foreign capital in gross fixed investment translates into a 10 per cent contribution to such growth. But for a variety of reasons, this is likely to underestimate the true impact. First, the concept of net material product is narrower than that of GDP, and use of the latter would reveal further additions to income growth, associated with FDI in such forms as the construction of tourist hotels and recreational facilities. Second, the most potent—albeit unquantifiable—contribution of FDI is probably concealed in our earlier finding that *productivity improvements* were the source of 53 per cent of net material product growth between 1986 and 1992. Finally, FDI has also served provincial economic development through its ability to ease foreign exchange constraints—a point taken up in the next section.

FOREIGN TRADE AS A CATALYST OF GROWTH[23]

Dramatic as the expansion of China's foreign trade has been since the inception of the Open Door strategy, the pace of growth in Guangdong has been even more spectacular.[24] As shown in Table 5.10, the provincial share of national exports rose from 12 to 22 per cent between 1980 and 1992. By the end of 1993, it had reached 29 per cent.[25] The increase in its import share, from less than 2 per cent to 14 per cent, was no less impressive.

The massive, widening gap between national and provincial trade ratios during the reform period reveals the spectacular nature of Guangdong's foreign trade growth. In Guangdong, the combined value of exports and imports as a proportion of GNP increased from 16 to 71 per cent between 1980 and 1992, compared with figures of 13 and 38 per cent for China. Even allowing for distortions in the data,[26] there can be no doubt that Guangdong has become the most open province in the country.

Table 5.9 Realized Intake of Foreign Capital in China and Guangdong, 1985–1992

| | Foreign Direct Investment | | | All Foreign Capital | | |
	National	GD	Ratio (%) (2)/(1)	National	GD	Ratio (%) (5)/(4)
	(1)	(2)	(3)	(4)	(5)	(6)
1985	16.61	5.15	31.01	46.47	9.19	19.78
1986	18.74	6.44	34.36	72.58	14.28	19.67
1987	23.14	5.94	25.67	84.52	12.17	14.40
1988	31.94	9.19	28.77	102.26	24.40	23.86
1989	33.92	11.56	34.08	100.59	23.99	23.85
1990	34.87	14.60	41.87	102.89	20.23	19.66
1991	43.66	18.23	41.75	115.54	25.82	22.35
1992	110.07	35.52	32.27	192.02	48.61	25.32
1985–92	312.95	106.63	34.07	816.87	178.69	21.87

Realized Intake (US$100 million)

Contributions to Fixed to Capital Formation (%)

	Foreign Direct Investment			All Foreign Capital		
	National	GD	Ratio (8)/(7)	National	GD	Ratio (11)/(10)
	(7)	(8)	(9)	(10)	(11)	(12)
1985	1.92	8.20	4.27	5.37	14.64	2.72
1986	2.14	10.26	4.79	8.29	22.76	2.74
1987	2.36	8.80	3.72	8.64	18.04	2.09
1988	2.64	9.67	3.66	8.46	25.67	3.03
1989	3.08	12.51	4.06	9.14	25.97	2.84
1990	3.75	18.73	5.00	11.05	25.95	2.35
1991	4.22	20.28	4.81	11.16	28.72	2.57
1992	7.73	21.25	2.75	13.48	29.08	2.16
1985–92	4.07	15.99	3.93	10.17	25.74	2.53

Notes: All US dollar figures are converted into yuan, by using the official annual average exchange rate, to be related to all fixed assets investment expenditure to arrive at the percentage contribution figures.
'All foreign capital' covers FDI, foreign borrowings, and other types of foreign investment.

Sources: Columns 1 and 4: ZGTJNJ 1993, p. 647.
Columns 2 and 5: GDTJNJ 1991, p. 316; 1993, p. 363.
Columns 7 to 12: Table 8 for the underlying fixed assets investment figures.
Exchange rates used for conversion: Nicholas R. Lardy, 'Chinese Foreign Trade', The China Quarterly, vol. 131, p. 706, Table 6; and ZGTJNJ 1993, p. 646.

Table 5.10 Exports, Imports, and Trade Ratios of China and Guangdong, 1978–1992

	Exports (US$100 million)			Imports (US$100 million)			Trade/Ratio (%)			
							Exports		Imports	
	National	GD	Ratio (%) (2)/(1)	National	GD	Ratio (%) (5)/(4)	National	GD	National	GD
	(1)	(2)	(3)	(4)	(5)	(6)	(7)	(8)	(9)	(10)
1978	97.5	13.88	14.24	108.9	2.04	1.87	4.67	12.62	5.22	1.85
1979	136.6	17.02	12.46	156.7	2.43	1.55	5.30	12.74	6.08	1.82
1980	181.2	21.95	12.11	200.2	3.56	1.78	6.07	13.40	6.68	2.17
1981	220.1	23.73	10.78	220.2	6.65	3.02	7.70	14.27	7.70	4.00
1982	223.2	22.56	10.11	192.9	8.01	4.15	7.97	12.87	6.88	4.57
1983	222.3	23.85	10.73	213.9	9.31	4.35	7.55	13.21	7.26	5.16
1984	261.4	24.87	9.51	274.1	11.17	4.08	8.34	13.12	8.91	5.89
1985	273.5	29.53	10.80	422.5	24.26	5.74	9.45	15.70	14.70	12.98

1986	309.4	42.51	13.74	429.0	25.58	5.96	11.16	23.00	15.45	13.84
1987	394.4	54.44	13.80	432.2	36.28	8.39	13.01	25.07	14.28	16.71
1988	475.2	74.84	15.75	552.8	51.10	9.24	12.56	25.34	12.56	17.30
1989	525.4	81.86	15.58	591.4	48.31	8.17	12.23	23.41	13.76	13.85
1990	620.9	105.60	17.01	533.5	57.49	10.78	16.87	34.30	14.55	27.64
1991	718.4	136.88	19.05	637.9	85.10	13.34	18.91	40.90	16.80	33.40
1992	850.0	184.40	21.69	806.1	111.79	13.87	19.41	44.34	18.49	26.88
Average:										
1978–85	201.98	22.17	10.98	223.68	8.43	3.77	7.25	13.57	8.05	5.16
1986–92	556.24	97.22	17.48	568.99	59.38	10.44	15.13	32.32	15.13	21.59

Notes: Figures for Guangdong 1978–80 include Hainan, which became an independent province in 1986.
National trade figures for 1978–79 are from the Ministry of Foreign Economic Relations and Trade; from 1980 onwards they are Customs statistics.
US Dollar figures are converted into Yuan, by using the official annual average exchange rate, to be related to the GNP/GDP in yuan to arrive at the trade ratio.
Instead of GNP, GDP is used as base for Guangdong's trade ratio.

Sources: Columns 1, 4, and 7: *ZGTJNJ 1993*, pp. 31 and 633.
Columns 2, 5, and 8: *GDTJNJ 1991*, pp. 57 and 303; *1993*, pp. 77 and 349; and *QJZDGD 1949–88*, p. 182.
Columns 3, 6, and 9: *ZGTJNJ 1993*, p. 646.
Exchanges rates used for conversion: Lardy, N. R., 'Chinese Foreign Trade', in *The China Quarterly*, vol. 131, p. 706 (Table 6); and *ZGTJNJ 1993*, p. 646.

In the absence of sophisticated input-output analysis, it is difficult to quantify precisely foreign trade's contribution to GNP growth in Guangdong. Instead, we offer the following estimates (admittedly, based on highly aggregative measures) as pointers to the changing role of the external sector since the beginning of the 1980s (Table 5.11).

The figures suggest that in the first half of the 1980s, the *pattern*, though not the absolute values, of the relative contributions of exports and domestic demand to GDP growth were similar in Guangdong and China. During the latter 1980s, however, the situation changed. The direction of such changes was the same,[27] but the strength with which they occurred was not. As a result, by the beginning of the 1990s, the role of exports dominated GDP growth in a way unparalleled throughout the country as a whole. To state the same point differently, Guangdong's GDP growth had become increasingly export-led during the 1980s.

Most FDI is export-orientated and the role which such investment has played in the export-led economic expansion of Guangdong has been correspondingly important. The figures in Table 5.12 show, for example, that FDI-related exports (including commissioned export processing, most of it on behalf of Hong Kong entrepreneurs) accounted for half of Guangdong's total exports in 1992, compared with a mere 17 per cent in 1985.[28]

Most FDI has been directed towards light industrial manufacturing activities. It therefore comes as no surprise to find that between 1980 and 1992, the combined share of light industrial goods and textiles in total provincial exports should have risen from 32 to 58 per cent (see Table 5.13). During the same period, the share of farm-related exports fell from 41 to 23 per cent.

The changing commodity composition of exports revealed in Table 5.13 reflects changes in the level of economic development in Guangdong. It is a commonplace that industrialization brings about fundamental structural change, as an economy shifts from primary product (especially agricultural) domination to a new stage, characterized by an expansion of

Table 5.11 Contributions of Exports, Imports, and Domestic Demand to Gross Domestic Product (GDP) Growth in China and Guangdong, Compared, 1981–1990 (in per cent)

	Growth of GDP			Contributions to the Growth of GDP								
				Exports			Imports			Domestic Demand		
	National	GD	Ratio (2)/(1)	National	GD	Ratio (5)/(4)	National	GD	Ratio (8)/(7)	National (1)−(4)−(7)	GD (2)−(5)−(8)	Ratio (11)/(10)
	(1)	(2)	(3)	(4)	(5)	(6)	(7)	(8)	(9)	(10)	(11)	(12)
1981	4.45	8.20	1.84	1.91	2.62	1.37	−1.26	−2.30	1.82	3.80	7.88	2.07
1982	8.49	11.50	1.35	1.51	1.75	1.16	−0.82	−2.12	2.66	7.78	11.87	1.53
1983	10.18	6.39	0.63	1.58	3.59	2.27	−3.05	−2.46	0.81	11.65	5.26	0.45
1984	14.58	14.78	1.01	2.69	3.48	1.29	−4.32	−2.90	0.67	16.21	14.20	0.88
1985	12.93	19.56	1.51	5.11	11.05	2.16	−14.25	−17.49	1.23	22.07	26.00	1.18
1986	8.51	11.19	1.32	7.27	22.86	3.14	−4.69	−5.47	1.17	5.93	−6.20	−1.05
1987	11.10	17.37	1.56	5.41	12.80	2.37	−2.52	−13.89	5.52	8.21	18.46	2.25
1988	11.28	15.23	1.35	2.19	12.13	5.54	−0.06	−3.61	56.11	9.15	6.71	0.73
1989	4.34	6.97	1.61	0.72	1.60	2.23	2.15	6.06	2.82	1.47	−0.57	−0.39
1990	3.73	11.21	3.01	11.02	30.73	2.79	−7.12	−18.10	2.54	−0.16	−1.52	9.76
Average												
1981–85	10.07	11.99	1.19	2.61	4.66	1.79	−5.13	−5.83	1.14	12.59	13.16	1.05
1986–90	7.74	12.34	1.59	5.51	16.38	2.97	−2.50	−7.14	2.86	4.73	3.10	0.66

Notes: All value figures are in 1980 constant prices.
See D. H. Perkins, 'Reforming China's economic system', *Journal of Economic Literature*, vol. 26 No. 2 (June 1988), pp. 628–9 for method of deriving the implicit deflators of GDP.
The exports (X) and imports (M) price indexes from the *Chinese Yearbook of Foreign Economic Relation and Trade 1991*, p. 321 are used for deflating both the national and Guangdong's trade figures
Contributions of X and M to GDP growth are estimated as: absolute change of X (or M)/absolute change of GDP, annual growth rate of GDP.
Sources: Tables 5.2 and 5.10.

Table 5.12 Foreign Direct Investment-related Exports and Imports of Guangdong Province, 1980–1992

	Commissioned Exports Processing		Compensation Trade		FDI-related Exports (US$ million) FDI Ventures		Total Value		FDI-related Imports (US$ million) FDI Ventures	
	Value	Share (%)	Value	Share (%)	Value	Share (%)	Value (1) + (3) + (5)	Share (%) (2) + (4) + (6)	Value	Share (%)
	(1)	(2)	(3)	(4)	(5)	(6)	(7)	(8)	(9)	(10)
1980	82.33	3.75	6.65	0.30	—	—	88.98	4.05	—	—
1985	272.5	9.23	8.70	0.29	22.16	7.49	303.36	17.01	336.56	13.87
1989	578.17	7.10	62.67	0.77	2,276.71	27.90	2,917.55	35.77	1,950.92	40.40
1990	583.32	5.52	77.78	0.74	3,723.83	35.26	4,384.93	41.52	3,297.44	57.36
1991	799.72	5.84	95.06	0.69	5,327.48	38.93	6,222.26	45.46	4,513.02	53.03
1992	999.23	5.42	96.69	0.52	8,159.06	44.25	9,254.98	50.19	6,014.96	53.80

Notes: All figures in columns 2, 4, 6, and 8 refer to the percentage shares in total exports; and similarly, figures in column 10 are percentage shares in total imports. The other components of Guangdong province's total exports (other than FDI-related exports) as implied in columns 1 and 8, are commodity exports (see Table 13).

Sources: GDTJNJ 1991, p. 304; 1993, p. 351.

Table 5.13 Composition of Commodity Exports of Guangdong Province, 1980–1992

| | Commodity Exports | | Commodity Export Composition (Total = 100%) | | | |
	Value (US$ million) (1)	Share in Total Exports (%) (2)	Farm & Subsidiary (3)	Farm Processing (4)	Light Industry & Textile (5)	Industrial and Minerals (6)
1980	2,105.74	95.95	31.50	9.80	32.12	26.58
1985	2,450.31	82.99	32.65	8.84	39.44	19.07
1989	5,250.12	64.20	19.40	7.60	53.10	19.90
1990	6,175.31	58.48	17.02	8.13	54.80	20.05
1991	7,465.61	54.45	16.60	7.40	55.67	20.33
1992	9,184.46	49.81	14.36	8.11	57.59	19.94

Notes: The declining trend of commodity exports reflects the growing importance of FDI-related exports as shown in Table 5.12.
Sources: GDTJNJ 1991, p. 304; 1993, p. 351.

manufacturing activities. Industrialization, of course, had been underway in Guangdong since the early 1950s. What is striking about post-1978 developments is the accelerated nature of the process and its emphasis on export-promotion rather than import-substitution.

SPECIAL ECONOMIC ZONES AND THE HONG KONG CONNECTION

No discussion of economic development in Guangdong can be considered complete without some reference to the SEZs[29] and the critical role played by Hong Kong. The preceding analysis has highlighted the enormous economic changes that have taken place from the perspective of the province as a whole. But further investigation of the regional dimension of these changes would reveal that the economic gains of the past fifteen years have been distributed unequally and skewed towards a few growth poles. These include the three original SEZs, Guangzhou, and several other municipalities, all of which were granted special economic privileges during the 1980s.[30] We have already investigated some aspects of the economic significance of such growth poles elsewhere.[31] In this section, we shall focus our attention on the role of the Guangdong–Hong Kong connection.

First, the role of Hong Kong as a source of capital: Table 5.14 reveals that Guangdong absorbed 42 per cent of all foreign direct investment flowing from Hong Kong into China during 1985 to 1992.[32] Viewed differently, Hong Kong was the immediate origin of 84 per cent of Guangdong's total FDI intake during the same period. If 'indirect' foreign investment (that is, capital borrowing from abroad) is included, the picture remains basically the same.

There is, however, an important qualification. Apart from several large-scale infrastructural projects (notably, the construction of the Guangzhou–Shenzhen highway and installation of major power-generation plants—all of them involving Hong Kong capital), a high proportion of FDI originating in Hong Kong reflects the relocation of manufacturing enterprises from the Territory to Guangdong (especially the Pearl River Delta).[33] A characteristic of such FDI is that it also generates trade flows. In other words, on the input side, the establishment of joint ventures normally involves the export of machinery and equipment, raw or semi-finished materials from Hong Kong to Guangdong; at the same time, most joint-venture output returns to Hong Kong for re-export to North America and Western Europe. It follows that most of Guangdong's FDI-related imports and exports have been, and still are, dominated by Hong Kong-based manufacturing firms operating within the province.

Table 5.15 gives a comprehensive picture of the role of Hong Kong in the foreign trade of both Guangdong and China as a whole since 1985. It shows an increasing trend in the provincial share of national exports to the Territory, reaching 41 per cent in 1992. In the same year, 84 per cent of Guangdong's exports were shipped to Hong Kong. Guangdong's dependence on its colonial neighbour for its imports also emerges clearly from Table 5.15.

Juxtaposition of the estimates of Guangdong's FDI-related exports and imports (Table 5.13) with the US dollar estimates of total provincial trade (Table 5.15) reveals that trade relations with Hong Kong reflect much more than investment in the Pearl River Delta. Clearly, non-FDI-related trade flows between Guangdong and Hong Kong are sizeable and have increased in recent years. No doubt a major contributory factor has been the need, against the background of accelerated export-based industrialization, to make use of Hong Kong's well-established port facilities, banking and financial services, telecommunications networks, and marketing skills in order to expand into international export markets. Hence the spectacular increases in Hong Kong's re-exports of goods of Chinese origin during the past decade.[34] The advantages of Hong Kong's international links and sourcing skills have no doubt similarly contributed to the surge in non-FDI-related *imports* through Hong Kong into Guangdong since the beginning of the 1990s.

In short, Hong Kong has been critical in transforming

Table 5.14 Hong Kong's Share in Realized Intake of Foreign Capital in China and Guangdong, 1985–1992

	Foreign Direct Investment					
	Total From Hong Kong (US$ million)			HK's Share in Total Intake (%)		
	National (1)	GD (2)	Ratio (%) (3)	National (4)	GD (5)	Ratio (%) (6)
1985	955.68	450.20	47.11	48.86	87.37	178.82
1986	1,328.71	603.10	45.39	59.22	93.66	158.16
1987	1,809.05	502.67	27.79	68.35	84.63	123.82
1988	2,428.05	836.54	34.45	64.93	91.02	140.18
1989	2,341.77	952.72	40.68	62.06	82.38	132.74
1990	2,118.48	1,018.59	48.08	56.42	69.77	123.66
1991	2,661.81	1,448.60	54.42	57.04	79.47	139.32
1992	7,908.94	3,162.27	39.98	70.04	89.04	127.13
1985–92	21,552.49	8,974.69	41.64	63.80	84.17	131.93

All Foreign Capital

	Total From Hong Kong (US$ million)			HK's Share in Total Intake (%)		
	National (7)	GD (8)	Ratio (%) (9)	National (10)	GD (11)	Ratio (%) (12)
1985	1,016.37	845.63	83.20	21.87	92.02	420.71
1986	1,572.85	1,095.45	69.65	21.67	76.71	353.99
1987	2,091.24	884.09	42.28	24.74	72.65	293.60
1988	3,109.44	1,537.96	49.46	30.41	63.03	207.29
1989	2,912.78	1,544.89	53.04	28.96	64.40	222.39
1990	2,431.68	1,298.76	53.41	23.63	64.20	271.64
1991	2,924.96	1,724.80	58.97	25.32	66.80	263.87
1992	8,689.95	3,623.25	41.69	45.26	74.54	164.70
1985–92	24,749.27	12,554.83	50.73	30.30	70.26	231.90

Notes: All investment figures refer to realized intake from both Hong Kong and Macau.
Sources: Columns 1, 4, 7, and 10: *ZGTJN/ 1986*, p. 580; *1987*, p. 604; *1988*, p. 734; *1989*, p. 646; *1991*, p. 630; and *1992*, p. 648.
Columns 2, 5, 8, and 11: *GDTJN/ 1991*, pp. 317 and 321; and *1993*, pp. 364 and 368.
Columns 4, 5, 10, and 11: Table 9.

Table 5.15 Hong Kong's role in the Foreign Trade of China and Guangdong, 1985–1992

	Exports to Hong Kong					
	Value (US$100 million)			Percentage Share		
	National	GD	Ratio (%) (2)/(1)	National	GD	Ratio (%) (5)/(4)
	(1)	(2)	(3)	(4)	(5)	(6)
1985	72.04	21.27	29.53	26.34	72.03	273.46
1986	97.85	29.55	30.20	31.63	69.51	219.80
1987	137.78	37.51	27.22	34.93	68.90	197.23
1988	182.69	57.25	31.34	38.44	76.50	198.98
1989	219.16	63.66	29.05	41.71	77.77	186.43
1990	266.50	85.43	32.06	42.92	80.90	188.48
1991	321.37	113.69	35.38	44.73	83.06	185.67
1992	375.12	155.58	41.47	44.13	84.37	191.18
1985–92	1,672.51	563.94	33.72	40.14	79.42	197.89

Imports from Hong Kong

	Value (US$100 million)			Percentage Share		
	National	GD	Ratio (%) (8)/(7)	National	GD	Ratio (%) (11)/(10)
	(7)	(8)	(9)	(10)	(11)	(12)
1985	47.97	21.43	44.67	11.35	88.33	778.02
1986	56.00	18.74	33.46	13.05	73.26	561.23
1987	84.37	28.95	34.31	19.52	79.80	408.77
1988	119.73	40.89	34.15	21.66	80.02	369.45
1989	125.40	34.97	27.89	21.20	72.39	341.38
1990	142.58	41.16	28.87	26.73	71.60	267.89
1991	174.63	62.30	35.68	27.38	73.21	267.42
1992	205.34	82.68	40.26	25.48	73.96	290.29
1985–92	956.02	331.12	34.64	21.70	75.27	346.83

Notes: Columns 4, 5, 10, and 11 show Hong Kong's percentage shares in total export and import volumes of China and Guangdong provinces, respectively.
Sources: Columns 1, 4, 7, and 10: *ZGTJNJ 1987*, p. 594; *1989*, p. 636; *1991*, p. 620; and *1993*, p. 638.
Columns 2, 5, 8, and 11: *GDTJNJ 1987*, p. 334; *1989*, p. 334; *1991*, p. 305; and *1993*, p. 352.
Columns 4, 5, 10, and 11: See sources of Table 5.10.

Guangdong into a major Chinese export base. It also promises to make the single most important contribution to fulfilling Guangdong's aspiration to become the fifth East Asian dragon.

THE ROLE OF THE STATE AND PROSPECTS FOR SUSTAINED GROWTH IN GUANGDONG

The state has already made a significant contribution to Guangdong's recent economic transformation and it will no doubt continue to be a critical determinant of the economic future of the province. We suggested earlier some of the factors which contributed to the rising share of the state-owned sector in provincial gross fixed investment during the 1980s. Large-scale infrastructural projects apart, there is a widespread presumption that economic activities conducted under the aegis of state ownership are inherently inefficient and should be phased out. Condemnation of this kind, however, is too facile and may deflect attention from other more important considerations. In Guangdong, one of these is the increasing extent to which state industrial enterprises, as well as Sino-foreign joint ventures, have become market-orientated. In this context—and against the background of an economic system which before 1978 was characterized by excessive centralized control and bureaucratic inertia—the distinction between different forms of ownership may be less significant than the efficiency-enhancing effects of greater competition.

Caution is needed in using the ratio between state budget and GNP as an accurate measure of the state's involvement in economic activities. The early stage of development is likely to be characterized by an increase in government spending in support of infrastructural construction. Subsequently, consumer pressures and demands for better social welfare shift government expenditure increasingly towards 'non-productive' investment in such areas as health, education, and housing. Both categories of expenditure necessarily imply a higher state budget share in GNP, even though the direct implications of each for economic growth may be very different.

In any case, the experience of Guangdong since 1978 in these regards is less than impressive. The estimates in Table 5.16 show that as a proportion of GNP, the combined total of state budgetary revenue and expenditure in Guangdong (for that matter, China too) generally declined after 1978. In both cases, this trend reflects the impact of widespread decentralization. Prior to 1978, under the system of Soviet-style, centralized planning, the state budget was a comprehensive financial instrument. That is, it not only embraced the financing of fixed investment and working capital requirements, but also provided for recurrent expenditure on non-productive items such as education, health, and national defence. Implicit in such financial arrangements was a system of compulsory profit remittances to the state budget, side by side with pervasive price and wage-fixing designed to allow the state to siphon off income in excess of subsistence needs.

Amongst the reforms initiated after 1978 were the introduction of a profit-retention scheme for state enterprises and the implementation of measures designed to decontrol wages and prices. These initiatives were bound to impact on existing financial arrangements and, as Table 5.16 shows, both nationally and in Guangdong the state budget/GNP ratio fell sharply. Although relatively speaking, the degree of budgetary curtailment was almost the same in Guangdong as in the country as a whole,[35] in reality the provincial impact was more severe because of its low base ratio of revenue/expenditure to GNP in 1978.[36]

Guangdong's budget/GNP ratio has also been consistently lower than the national average for the years under study.[37] Unlike Shanghai and Liaoning, Guangdong has not been subject to enforced, large-scale financial transfers by the centre. The inference is that the budgetary privileges extended to the provincial authorities by Beijing have helped remove excessive fiscal obligations from industries under their jurisdiction. In this way, industrial incentives have been significantly enhanced.

Nevertheless, at the beginning of the 1990s, Guangdong's budget/GNP ratio was significantly lower than that of many

185

Table 5.16 Budgetary Ratio of China and Guangdong, 1978–1992 (in per cent)

	Revenue/GNP			Expenditure/GNP			Total Budget/GNP		
	National	GD	Ratio (2)/(1)	National	GD	Ratio (5)/(4)	National	GD	Ratio
	(1)	(2)	(3)	(4)	(5)	(6)	(7)	(8)	(9)
1978	33.75	21.36	0.63	30.97	14.63	0.47	64.72	35.99	0.56
1980	24.28	14.69	0.61	27.13	10.15	0.37	51.41	24.84	0.48
1985	21.81	11.84	0.54	21.56	11.00	0.51	43.37	22.84	0.53
1986	23.31	12.92	0.55	24.04	14.04	0.58	47.35	26.96	0.57
1987	20.96	11.50	0.55	21.67	11.13	0.51	42.63	22.63	0.53
1988	18.68	9.79	0.52	19.24	10.49	0.55	37.92	20.28	0.53
1989	18.43	10.43	0.57	19.01	10.76	0.57	37.44	21.19	0.57
1990	18.72	8.90	0.48	19.51	10.24	0.52	38.23	19.14	0.50
1991	17.84	9.96	0.56	18.85	10.25	0.54	36.69	20.21	0.55
1992	17.28	9.71	0.56	18.26	9.58	0.52	35.54	19.29	0.54

Notes: For Guangdong province GDP, rather than GNP, is used as base for the respective ratios.
Total budget refers to the combined total of revenue and expenditure.

Sources: ZGTJNJ 1993, pp. 31 and 217 for national figures; and GDTJNJ 1987, p. 367; 1989, p. 367; 1993, p. 383 for Guangdong's figures.
See sources of Table 5.2 for the underlying GNP/GDP data.

developing countries—and certainly lower than that of each of the East Asian four dragons. This cannot simply be attributed to the impact of reform upon earlier excessive centralization. Rather, the relatively low ratio may reflect fiscal constraints on the capacity of the provincial government to involve itself in infrastructural construction and social welfare programmes.[38]

Such considerations counsel caution in predicting when, or even if, rising per capita GNP will enable Guangdong to set aside a major—and increasing—proportion of budgetary revenue in order to promote further growth and enhance social welfare.

This, in turn, begs the even more fundamental question of whether Guangdong can sustain the recent, powerful momentum of economic growth in the immediate future. Major projects currently under construction or in the planning stage—the Shenzhen–Guangzhou highway, the Yantian Port project, and the new international airport for Shantou, Jieyang, and Chaozhou cities—attest to the high level of confidence in the province. Indeed, given the broader background of the development experience of the four East Asian dragons, there is no reason why Guangdong should not maintain sufficient growth to fulfil its objectives. After all, South Korea's long-term GNP growth averaged only 8.6 per cent per annum in the 30 years after 1962—considerably less than that of Guangdong during the post-1978 reform period.[39] Barring any major unexpected disturbance—and even allowing for some slowing in provincial growth in the years to come—it seems reasonable to suppose that Guangdong's recent impressive record will, in the foreseeable future, enable it to emulate the successful performance of the other dragons since the 1960s.

There are, however, important qualifications to such a sanguine prognosis, two of which may be mentioned here. The first concerns the ability of Guangdong to maintain its recent growth momentum. Fulfilment of provincial GDP targets for the years 2000 and 2010 originally required average growth rates of 13.4 and 12.4 per cent per annum during the 1990s and the first decade of the next century.[40] It is true that average growth during the early 1990s remains well ahead of such requirements.[41] But some would argue that Guangdong is already close to a growth ceiling and that structural and other bottlenecks will make it increasingly difficult to maintain the recent momentum of development. Even official sources concede the existence of serious obstacles to modernization. The production structure remains irrational;[42] regional growth is still uneven;[43] heavy infrastructural capital requirements place a heavy burden on the provincial budget; and the technical and scientific base is weak.

The second qualification emerges from the earlier experience of the East Asian little dragons. The economic transformation of all four was a function of the sustained economic growth of advanced western countries (notably Japan and the United States). Japan, for example, provided large-scale imports of industrial equipment and raw materials; in addition, the United States and Western Europe provided markets for manufactured exports.[44] Whether the global economic environment will be conducive to the future growth requirements of the aspiring fifth dragon is a matter of judgement. But it is likely that through their impact upon Guangdong's exports, the US government and economy will continue significantly to influence its economic future. Even if the decision to delink the renewal of China's most-favoured-nation (MFN) status from political and human rights considerations marks a significant step forward, the uncertainty which still surrounds Sino-US relations highlights Guangdong's potential vulnerability from this source.

NOTES

1. During his tour of southern China [*nanxun*] between January and February 1992, Deng Xiaoping described Guangdong as the 'leading force for economic development' and explicitly urged the region to catch up with the 'four little dragons' during the next twenty years. See Robert F. Ash, 'Quarterly Chronicle and Documentation', *The China Quarterly* [hereafter *CQ*], 130 (June 1992): 455. The four dragons are South Korea, Taiwan, Hong Kong, and Singapore.
2. Lardy points out that by the mid-1980s, Guangdong 'was able to spend

most of its fiscal revenues', its quota for tax remission to the centre having been reduced from USD 1.0 to 0.772 billion between 1980–82 and 1986–90. See Nicholas R. Lardy, *Foreign Trade and Economic Reform in China, 1978–1990*, Cambridge: Cambridge University Press, 1992, pp. 55 and 135.

3. Shenzhen, Zhuhai, and Shantou SEZs were set up in Guangdong in 1980. The fourth SEZ was Xiamen in Fujian province.

4. Only South Korea, with a population of 43 million and a land mass of 0.099 million km², approaches it. Taiwan falls far behind, with a population one-third, and a surface area one-fifth of those of Guangdong. The city-states of Hong Kong and Singapore are of course minuscule by comparison.

5. See also Robert F. Ash and Y. Y. Kueh, 'Economic Integration within Greater China: Trade and Investment Flows between China, Hong Kong and Taiwan', *CQ*, 136, Table 11 and p. 743.

6. GDP growth averaged 9.0 per cent and 13.3 per cent per annum in China and Guangdong, respectively, between 1979 and 1992.

7. The figures are derived from the estimates of absolute GDP in Table 5.2 and of sectoral contributions to GDP in Table 5.5 They are consistent with Guangdong's shares in national GVIO and GVAO, shown in Table 5.2.

8. The disappointing performance of the grain sector in southern China (of which Guangdong is a part) is touched on in Robert F. Ash, 'The Agricultural Sector in China: Performance and Policy Dilemmas during the 1990s', *CQ*, 131 (September 1992): 575. By 1993–94, the urgency of the situation, associated in particular with a sharp decline in the grain sown area, was reflected in provincial government calls to prevent further loss of land and increase investment in order to restore levels of grain production.

9. GVAO embraces not only crop farming, but also fishing, animal husbandry, forestry, and subsidiaries. RSVO (rural social value-output) extends the coverage by including the value of production of rural industries.

10. In fairness, it should be said that with the exception of South Korea between 1986 and 1992, China also achieved faster growth than the four dragons during 1979 and 1992, and 1986 and 1992. But in the case of Guangdong, the gap was much narrower and the growth record of all five regions was in fact quite similar.

11. From 12 per cent to 15 per cent in aggregate terms; and from 10 per cent to 12 per cent in per capita terms.

12. In 1994 foreign capital still accounted for a significant proportion of total fixed capital formation in Guangdong.

13. Notice, however, that the process has been more pronounced in Guangdong than in the rest of the country—this, in turn, reflecting improved capital productivity rather than the use of more physical capital.

14. Guangdong's per capita growth performance also easily outpaced that of every one of the four dragons. See Table 5.3.

15. Between 1980 and 1992, the share of agriculture in total employment fell from 71 per cent to 47 per cent in Guangdong, and from 69 per cent to 59 per cent in China. During the same period, the employment share of industry increased from 17 per cent to 30 per cent (Guangdong), but from 18 per cent to 22 per cent (China); and in services from 12 per cent to 22 per cent (Guangdong), but from 13 per cent to 20 per cent (China).

16. Relevant data are available in Anis Chowdhury and Iyanatul Islam, *The Newly Industrialising Economies of East Asia*, London: Routledge, 1993, Tables 1.5 and 1.7.

17. A major part of the background to Guangdong's recent economic expansion has undoubtedly been increased inter-regional mobility within the province, as well as large-scale migration from outside in order to take advantage of employment opportunities. The associated pressures have contributed to the breakdown of administrative barriers (notably, the 'household registration' [*hukou*] system), which since the early 1950s had prevented large-scale rural–urban movements of population. They have also given rise to an enormous 'floating population' and many millions of 'illegal' or 'temporary' residents in major cities. To what extent these urban dwellers should be accorded proper urban entitlements and benefits is a major problem now facing the government. See *Ta Kung Pao* (Ta Kung Daily, hereafter *TKP*), Hong Kong, 16 January 1994, p. 2.

18. In numerical terms, the sources of improvements in productivity are a residual, left over after the relative contributions of physical increases in labour and capital to income growth have been isolated. Their verification at an aggregate level is not readily susceptible to econometric testing (especially if reference is made to X-efficiency considerations).

19. Foreign domestic investment (FDI) into Guangdong rose by 95 per cent in 1992 (but by 152 per cent in China); the corresponding figures for all foreign capital were 88 per cent and 66 per cent (see Table 5.9). In 1993, Guangdong's realized FDI and total foreign capital inflows increased, respectively, by a further 113 per cent and 75 per cent, to reach US\$6.2 billion and US\$8.5 billion. See *TKP*, 3 January 1994 and Table 5.9.

20. The prediction was made in Y. Y. Kueh, 'Foreign Investment and Economic Change in China', *CQ*, 132 (September 1992). By 1994, Guangdong's share of national FDI had fallen further to under 28 per cent (*ZGTJNJ* 1995, p. 557)

21. On the basis of inflows of *all* foreign capital, the figure is significantly higher—around 30 per cent during 1991 and 1992.

22. Kueh, 'Foreign Investment and Economic Change in China', p. 658. The combination of a stable US dollar and accelerated price inflation

in China in recent years suggests that the 3:1 ratio needs to be revised upwards.

23. A detailed analysis of Guangdong's foreign trade reforms and their impact is given by John Kamm, 'Reforming Foreign Trade', in Ezra F. Vogel, *One Step Ahead in China: Guangdong under Reform*, Cambridge, Mass.: Harvard University Press, 1989.

24. For detailed consideration of Guangdong's foreign trade since 1978, see Ash and Kueh, 'Economic Integration within Greater China'.

25. *TKP*, 3 January 1994.

26. The conversion of US dollar-based trade figures into renminbi in order to facilitate comparison with yuan-based GDP estimates is likely to exaggerate imports and exports under the impact of erratic yuan depreciations during the second half of the 1980s.

27. That is, both Guangdong and China experienced a relative rise in the contribution of export demand, but a relative decline in that of domestic demand.

28. For more detailed consideration of this aspect, see Ash and Kueh, 'Economic Integration within Greater China'.

29. A useful account of Guangdong's SEZs and their early experience is given in 'Special Economic Zones: Experiment in New Systems', in Vogel, *One Step Ahead in China*.

30. The three SEZs (Shenzhen, Zhuhai, and Shantou) were set up in 1980. In 1984, Guangzhou (the provincial capital) was included amongst the fourteen coastal cities designated by the central government to be opened to foreign investment. In 1988, several other major provincial municipalities were added to the list.

31. Kueh, 'Foreign Investment and Economic Change in China', and Ash and Kueh, 'Economic Integration within Greater China'.

32. Prior to 1985, the corresponding figure was even higher—a reflection of the even greater importance of Guangdong as a recipient of foreign capital.

33. Exorbitant increases in land rents and persistent labour shortages have prompted this transfer of manufacturing activity. In so doing, they have contributed to a complex process of de-industrialization, which has fundamentally changed the economic structure of Hong Kong. See Ash and Kueh, 'Economic Integration within Greater China', and Y. P. Ho and Y. Y. Kueh, 'Whither Hong Kong in an Open-Door, Reforming Chinese Economy?', *The Pacific Review* (London), 6, 4 (December 1993).

34. See Ho and Kueh, 'Whither Hong Kong?', p. 339.

35. This is demonstrated by estimates of the relationship between the ratio of total state budget (revenue and expenditure) to GNP in 1992 and 1978. The calculated figures are 0.54 for Guangdong and 0.55 for China.

36. In 1978, Guangdong's ratio of revenue (expenditure) to GNP was 21 per cent (15 per cent). The corresponding figures for China were 34 per cent (31 per cent).

37. In general, both the revenue/GNP and expenditure/GNP ratios for Guangdong were between 50 per cent and 60 per cent of the national figures after 1980.

38. Perhaps this also explains some of the less positive factors associated with recent reforms, such as severe urban traffic congestion, environmental pollution, and deteriorating medical services and health care.

39. Compare Table 5.3 and Kihwan Kim and Kwang Choi, 'Strategies for Structural Adjustment and Rapid Development in Korea', paper presented at the Western Economic Association International Pacific Rim Conference, 8–13 January 1994, Hong Kong.

40. These figures are taken from *Draft Programme for Economic and Social Development in Guangdong* (1990–2010), as cited in *TKP*, 22 February 1994.

41. Compare the following provincial annual growth rates: 1991, 14.3 per cent; 1992, 19.9 per cent; and 1993, 21 per cent (Table 5.3 and *TKP*, 22 February 1994).

42. Zhu Senlin himself has referred to internal irrationalities within Guangdong's agricultural and manufacturing sectors, as well as to the lagging performance of the tertiary sector. By 2010 the ratio of value-output of primary to secondary to tertiary sectors is planned to change from 26:40:34 (1990) to 5:31:64 (*TKP*, 22 February 1994).

43. The benefits of rapid provincial growth have accrued disproportionately to the three SEZs and the Pearl River Delta region.

44. This point was developed by Simon Kuznets in his assessment of Taiwan's modern economic transformation. See his 'Economic Growth and Structural Change' in W. Galenson (ed.), *Economic Development and Structural Change in Taiwan: The Postwar Experience of the Republic of China*, Ithaca: Cornell University Press, 1979.

INDEX

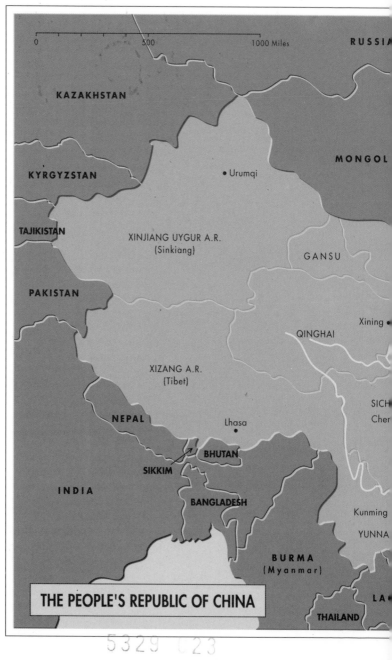

THE PEOPLE'S REPUBLIC OF CHINA